UNTANGLING
THE WEB

To my beautimus wife, Jessica. Thank you for Wasting your time with me.

Steve Dembo

*For my mom and dad who told me I could make the world a
better place and for my wonderful wife and amazing kids
who encourage me to try to do it.*

Adam Bellow

20 Tools
to Power Up
Your Teaching

UNTANGLING
THE WEB

Steve Dembo ⚙ **Adam Bellow**

CORWIN
A SAGE Company

CORWIN
A SAGE Company

FOR INFORMATION:

Corwin

A SAGE Company

2455 Teller Road

Thousand Oaks, California 91320

(800) 233-9936

www.corwin.com

SAGE Publications Ltd.

1 Oliver's Yard

55 City Road

London EC1Y 1SP

United Kingdom

SAGE Publications India Pvt. Ltd.

B 1/I 1 Mohan Cooperative Industrial Area

Mathura Road, New Delhi 110 044

India

SAGE Publications Asia-Pacific Pte. Ltd.

3 Church Street

#10-04 Samsung Hub

Singapore 049483

Acquisitions Editor: Arnis Burvikovs

Associate Editor: Desirée A. Bartlett

Editorial Assistant: Mayan N. White

Production Editor: Cassandra Margaret Seibel

Copy Editor: Megan Markanich

Typesetter: C&M Digitals (P) Ltd.

Proofreader: Susan Schon

Indexer: Will Ragsdale

Cover Designer: Michael Dubowe

Permissions Editor: Jennifer Barron

Printed in the United States of America

A catalog record of this book is available from the Library of Congress.

ISBN 978-1-4833-3320-5

This book is printed on acid-free paper.

SUSTAINABLE FORESTRY INITIATIVE
Certified Chain of Custody
Promoting Sustainable Forestry
www.sfiprogram.org
SFI-01268
SFI label applies to text stock

13 14 15 16 17 10 9 8 7 6 5 4 3 2 1

CONTENTS

PREFACE

This book is an introduction to the best online web tools for educators. It provides teachers with twenty sites (plus a few bonus ones) that will energize learning, foster collaboration, and infuse creativity throughout the curriculum.

Every tool in this book is either free or **freemium** (i.e., free, with optional upgrades available for a fee). The sites are flexible enough that they can be used by kindergarten students as easily as by twelfth graders, regardless of subject area. In addition to introductory activities and stretch ideas, we've included explanations of why they are relevant and some creative ways to use them. Throughout the book, you'll find quotes from dozens of leaders in the education community. Not only do you get the perspective of the authors but we are connecting you to mentors and colleagues who are eager to share their expertise with you.

Join us at the online community site at www.untanglingthewebcommunity.com, where you can connect and collaborate with other teachers who are reading this book and undertaking a similar educational journey. We will be participating in conversations there, both through discussion forums as well as through live events. This book is more than a how-to guide; it's your first step to leveraging new technologies to transform classroom experiences.

WHY WE WROTE THIS BOOK

Sharing tools and resources is something that we do on a regular basis. At conferences, through our websites, and using social media, we are constantly discovering, evaluating, and promoting tools that can be used in education. Considering our affinity for web-based technologies, it may seem strange that we decided to write a book. But the reality is, we have both found that as empowering as new technologies can be, many of us still learn best by using print as a reference and launching point. We felt that a book providing educators with a concise list of the best web tools available to them was something that could impact educators at a practical level. Our goal was not only to provide a starting point for each of those tools but to also have a bit of fun with it. Let's face it: If you are in education today, you must have a sense of humor!

There are several other books about **Web 2.0** out there, but they aren't ours. They don't have the specific tools we want to discuss, nor do they approach them in a way that we feel is relevant to educators today. We believe teaching should be fun, and these tools are all about combining engagement and empowerment with an element of play. We want teachers to feel comfortable infusing these web tools into their classrooms and lessons, and we want to see the great projects and ideas that are created with them.

On a personal level, we both are the parents of young children. From a purely selfish perspective, we want to see them grow up in a world where technology provides unique educational experiences that challenge them, inspire them, and foster a love of learning. We believe sharing our passion for new technologies with other educators is a means to facilitate that.

THE EVOLUTION OF THE WEB (ABRIDGED)

It all starts with Al Gore and the creation of the Internet (I'm kidding). What many consider *Web 1.0* was a static series of pages that users accessed and retrieved information from. Think back to the days of AOL and that lovely sound you would get while trying to connect to their interface for the Internet. Pages were informative but not interactive, and engagement was limited to reading or printing it.

But that all changed in the early 2000s. Interactivity came to the web. Instead of being passive consumers of content, we were able to craft content of our own, a trend that has exploded over the past decade.

This shift was so dramatic, and the ways we interacted with the medium so greatly altered, that people began to use the term *Web 2.0,* or the *Read/Write Web.* This era allowed the casual web user to shift from being an information consumer to a content producer.

While still sometimes referred to as Web 2.0, the term that was coined almost a decade ago has lost much of its relevance as we would be hard pressed to think of a site that lacked the basic functionality that the term refers to. A web tool is just that—a site on the web that is used actively to achieve a purpose for the user.

EVALUATING NEW TECHNOLOGIES

In this book, we have shared the sites that we feel are absolutely essential for every educator to know about. While they may not all be a perfect fit for you, they are representative of the genres of sites that are available—and just a few of many flavors. The specifics of each site may vary, but the broad ideas defining why they are significant are consistent from site to site.

The rate at which new sites have been released is absolutely dizzying. Every time you turn around, it seems there is a new site being heralded as the latest and greatest. While it is easy to get caught up in shiny new offerings, there are specific characteristics that determine just how appropriate they are for educators to invest their time (and money) in.

Upon visiting a new site, there are a few things to examine right off the bat. The first is to determine whether the site has an education-friendly portal, or educator accounts available. Many sites recognize that the general public may use their sites to create content that wouldn't be appropriate for a school setting. Education portals frequently address these concerns and provide additional features like student accounts or privacy settings not available through the primary version.

Once determining which version (if multiple are available) to evaluate, the next step is to assess what is being shared publicly. Sites that provide a gallery of recent content can be problematic for many educators. Since the content shared there is typically generated automatically, without moderation, there is a chance that inappropriate content will be visible to discourage educators from using the site at all. Along the same lines, educators should check to see if a global search exists, typically in the upper right corner of the page. If so, it would be prudent to search for terms that may tempt middle schoolers and see what results come up. Once again, the potential for discovering inappropriate content in this way may be a major deterrent to spending any time exploring further.

The next element to investigate is the registration process. Most sites do require users to sign in, but there are variations there. Sites that allow users to create without registering are highly desirable, as many schools forbid students from using personal e-mail accounts during school hours. Some sites, particularly those with education portals, may even allow teachers to set up registration codes for students, bypassing the need for them to go through an extensive registration process. These two scenarios are the best case, but many do require individual accounts for each student. This may not be prohibitive, but it is advisable to check their terms of service to ensure that there are no age restrictions preventing use by your students.

Another aspect of the site to consider is the option for publishing. Nearly every tool allows you to save content within the site itself; educators must check to see if students have the ability to save their work privately. Depending on the project, they may not want to publish their work to the world, and privacy options are critical. One option that has become popular of late is the ability to share globally—but only to those who are provided the link directly. The work isn't shared with others within the site, nor will it appear in search engines, but anyone who has the direct link will be able to access it. Beyond privacy, it is important to check how the content itself can be shared out. Many sites offer the ability to publish directly to popular video/image sharing sites or through social networks, but educators should always check to see if creations could be saved offline. Sharing online is valuable, but being able to save the work offline is critical, especially considering the shelf life of many websites today. Before committing to a site, consider your exit strategy. If you decide to stop using it, will you be able to take your content with you? If not, you may want to consider alternatives.

A final consideration, perhaps the most important one, is cost. One of the most appealing aspects of the online tool revolution is that so many sites are free. Then again . . . is anything truly free? These sites cost quite a bit to develop. And once they've been launched, there are maintenance costs, service costs, bandwidth costs, and much more. Lest we kid ourselves, creating and maintaining a site like the ones shared in this book is far from free. This is why so many sites have moved to a freemium model. This means that they provide a certain level of access for free and make available advanced features at a cost (flat or recurring). Other sites attempt to recoup the costs of maintaining the site by displaying ads to users, which may or may not be appropriate for students to view. While ads are hardly ideal for an educational setting, they may be more palatable than incurring a monthly fee. Sites that provide educator accounts typically remove the ads for those users, but this is not guaranteed. The one thing to keep in mind with respect to cost is that if you don't see a way for the site to make money (subscriptions, premium features, ads, etc.), be aware that the site may not be around for the long haul. There are always exceptions, but if a site isn't making money, it is probably losing it. And sites that lose money may not be there the next time you take your students to the computer lab.

WHAT MAKES THIS BOOK SPECIAL

Traditionally, books are individual experiences. This book is not intended to be used that way.

This is not a textbook, nor is it a traditional reference volume. While we have aggregated common sites together, that does not mean they represent a specific progression from one to the next. Each tool within this book represents a launching point. We will share our thoughts about why each technology is significant and a few ideas for getting your feet wet. At that point, though, it is up to you to dive in. There are too many variations to create a comprehensive list of all the ways to use them. Even if we devoted an entire book to each site, we would still encounter people who were left unaccounted for. More than likely, the specific lesson ideas we've shared will not apply perfectly to you. What we expect is that you will use those as inspiration and consider how they can be adapted to meet your own needs.

We have been fortunate enough to be connected to a community of inspiring educators. One of our goals in this book was to share their ideas with you. Every site in the book features quotes, ideas, and testimonials from educators who are evangelists for it. We've included their Twitter name so that if you have further questions, you have a resource you can connect with. The idea isn't just to see the faces of educators that are making use of these sites but to add them to your own network and leverage them as the need arises.

We also decided to create our own community that focuses on the topics that you will be exploring as you work your way through this book. You, as a proud owner of *Untangling the Web,* are encouraged to join us online at the *Untangling the Web* community site at www.untanglingthewebcommunity.com. In addition to in-text step-by-step guides, we have created video tutorials for each of the 20 featured web tools. You can access these ☐ **See Tool in Action** tutorials either by clicking on the video screen shot, activating the QR code, or visiting the community site. We hope you will join us and share your ideas for using these powerful web tools in schools.

There is no substitute for experience. And your experiences will be unique to you. This is why the community elements are so critical not only to your own success but to those you will be sharing with. Start with the ideas we've documented here. Discover the variations of them that suit your own needs. Share those variations with the community, and let others benefit from your learning.

Read. Explore. Share.

NOTE FROM THE PUBLISHER

If you purchased the interactive eBook version of this text, you have received a brochure with an access code and special instructions about how to get started. If you did not purchase the interactive eBook, you can still gain access to all of the same online resources referenced in the text by visiting the online community at www.untanglingthewebcommunity.com.

HOW TO ACCESS THE FEATURES
OF THE INTERACTIVE EBOOK

Once you have logged in to the interactive eBook, follow the directions below:

- Click on ▢ **See Tool in Action** screen shots to view video tutorials
- Roll over bolded words to view definitions
- Click on underlined words and phrases to link out to additional information
- Click on Tweeters' Twitter handles to visit their Twitter pages

You can also access the video tutorials, key term definitions, and links by visiting the online community at www.untanglingthewebcommunity.com.

▢ See the Authors in Action

ICON KEY

 Free

 Freemium

 Mobile Compatible

 May Contain Objectionable Content

 Printable

 Under 5 Minutes

 No Registration Required

 Educator Version

ABOUT THE AUTHORS

 As a former kindergarten teacher and school Director of Technology **Steve Dembo** is a pioneer in the field of educational social networking. Currently serving as Discovery Education's Director of Social Media Strategy and Online Community, Dembo was among the first educators to realize the power of blogging, podcasting, Twitter, and other Web 2.0 technologies in connecting educators and creating professional learning communities.

In 2010, the National School Board Association named Dembo one of "Twenty to Watch," a list honoring individuals finding innovative ways to use technology to increase classroom learning. His work with the Discovery Educator Network has earned an Award of Excellence from Technology and Learning magazine, a Distinguished Achievement Award for Instructional Website from the Association of Educational Publishers, a BESSIE Award for Best Professional Development Website, and the Best in Tech award for Professional Development and Resource Solutions by Scholastic Administrator magazine.

Steve Dembo is a course designer and adjunct professor for Wilkes University where he serves as class instructor for the Internet Tools for Teaching course within the Instructional Media degree program. He has delivered keynote and featured presentations at conferences around the world including ISTE, TCEA, FETC, MACUL, CUE, ICE, #140Edu and TEDxCorpusChristi.

Steve lives in Skokie, IL with his wife Jessica and two children, Aiden and Ruby. He currently serves on the school board for Skokie-Morton Grove School District 69. Weekends, he dresses up as a TIE Fighter Pilot and does charity work with the 501st Legion. #TrueStory

Adam Bellow is one of today's leading speakers on educational technology and infusing technology to aid school reformation. He is the founder of both eduTecher and eduClipper. In addition to these free resources, Adam launched the popular student-focused social charity campaign, *Change the World.*

Bellow began his career teaching High School English for students with language-based learning disabilities. While going for his first master's degree, he was asked to teach the graduate level course for his peers on the value of Technology for the Special Education Classroom based on his clear passion for the subject. It was during this course that he created a resource for his students called eduTecher, which grew to become one of the most widely heralded and respected hubs to learn about free web tools for the K–12 landscape. eduTecher launched the first mobile applications for educational technology.

In 2007 Bellow became a technology training specialist for a school district and worked daily with hundreds of teachers across K–12 to help them better infuse technology into their classrooms. In 2010 he began working as the Director of Educational Technology for the College Board Schools and later served as the Senior Director of Educational Technology for the AP Program.

Bellow was honored by ISTE in 2010 as an emerging leader and then again in 2011 when he was named Outstanding Young Educator of the year.

Bellow has been a sought after speaker in the education and educational technology circuit over the past few years because of his particular high-speed delivery which blends humor and rapid fire visuals in a style that re-defines slide-aided presentation. Among other conferences, he has keynoted/presented at ISTE, TEDxNYED, and #140edu.

Bellow is currently serving as CEO of eduClipper, the edtech startup that he founded in 2012. eduClipper is a free web tool focused on helping students and teachers find, share, and build valid learning experiences in a K–12 safe educational social platform. He is happily married and has two wonderful boys.

1

CURATION TOOLS

Where Did I Put That Awesome Resource?

Do you remember stepping into a classroom for the first time? Inexperienced, more than a little nervous, and anxiously wondering if you had the skills and resources to lead a class of students through the upcoming learning journey? And then opening up the file cabinet to find that the previous teacher had miraculously left their entire collection of handouts, lesson plans, and resources for you to find. Your sigh of relief was only slightly eclipsed by the resounding John Williams-esque soundtrack you could hear in your own ears. It is the educational equivalent of discovering a chest of gold buried in your own yard.

Even just a few short years ago, the primary way that people shared resources was by photocopying them and passing them along, hand to hand. Finding quality resources online was arduous at best. The reason for this wasn't because people weren't interested in sharing but because the tools to do so hadn't evolved enough to make it simple and unobtrusive. Some people may be motivated to spend large amounts of time sorting through resources and sharing them out, but most people will only do it if it is convenient. We have a finite amount of time and have to prioritize it to best suit our individual needs.

Not long after the introduction of **blogs,** Joshua Schechter founded a simple website called Del.icio.us. It provided a means for people to save their bookmarks (or favorites) online and access them from any one of the many computers people might use. There were several other ways to address this problem, but Del.icio.us made one additional change that distinguished it from the others prior to it; user bookmarks were shared publicly. Essentially, it enabled people to practice the same behavior they always had (saving websites), but without any further effort on their part, they could share their discoveries out with others. In a sense, they took their file drawers of resources and opened them up to the world.

This fundamentally changed the hunt-and-gather experience for users. Previously, when people sought and saved resources, they did so only to their own benefit. Now, other users could navigate to their resources and reap the rewards of their efforts. This added an extrinsic reward (recognition) in addition to the intrinsic. It also removed the technical barriers to gathering and sharing resources online, opening it up to a much wider swath of users.

The introduction of these new **curation** tools coincided with the explosive onset of the information era. Blogs, podcasts, and wikis dramatically increased the amount of content for people to sift through, and **social bookmarking** tools like Delicious (now renamed), and Diigo allowed users to collect, organize, and share out what they found. As the number of resources increased, the need for new methods of organization arose. Traditionally, organization was taxonomy based. Hierarchical categories using a fixed vocabulary was efficient when just a few people were responsible for creating the organizational structure. However, when each user became responsible for creating their own method of organization, taxonomies gave way to a new method of categorization. Folksonomies, also known as free tagging, depended on the individual to associate keywords to each resource they saved. These tags were completely individualized, relying on the user's own experiences and associations to determine the relevance of the vocabulary used. While the specific keywords may vary wildly from user to user, when aggregated in groups, trends tended to emerge. For example, while some people may tag CNN.com with *morning routine,* the majority of users who bookmarked it would add the keyword *news.* In this way, while folksonomies may never be 100 percent accurate or comprehensive, they make up for it through their efficiency, essentially democratizing the organization of resources.

The result of these changes was that resource sharing became personalized but less private. The web allowed us to curate content for ourselves as we saw fit but at the same time benefit from the efforts of a larger community. Curation started as a means to organize one's own resources, while having some benefit to others in the process. Gradually, people began sifting through the hordes of resources available solely to pay it forward, knowing that their efforts would be of great benefit to others who were searching for similar things. Much like museum curators, people who organized classroom resources, along with detailed supplemental information, created a destination for explorers on the web looking for new ideas. Whether they were doing it for their own benefit or for the sake of others, lists of resources began to be as sought after as the resources themselves.

Today, curation tools have evolved far beyond simply lists of links. Some are 100 percent visual in nature; others provide advanced features such as page caching, group collaboration, and a variety of publication methods. The idea behind them (gathering and sharing resources) remains consistent; the flavors are incredibly diverse. People often ask, "Which tool should I use to save my websites?" The answer to that is as complex as trying to determine which car is the best for a person. It all depends on what the user's specific needs are. Someone who wants to save sites to use as a dashboard for their elementary students would need a very different site than someone who would like to organize bulletin board ideas to share with their colleagues. A high school social studies teacher may seek out a site that allows students to organize their online research as a group while a school principal may want to aggregate inspiring videos related to an upcoming policy change. At the core, these are all similar activities, but the specifics will dictate which site would best suit their needs.

In this chapter, we've gathered three of the very best curation sites available to educators. This list is far from comprehensive though, and, based on your own needs, you may find a better fit outside the list we have selected. However, by exploring the sites listed here, you'll gain a strong understanding of the types of curation sites that are out there and where their strengths lie. At the end of the day, it all comes down to determining what you want to save and how or with whom you want to share it that will determine your ideal match.

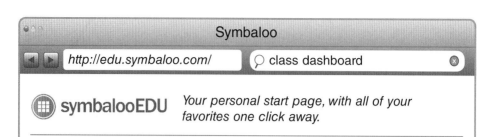

http://edu.symbaloo.com/   class dashboard

 symbalooEDU   *Your personal start page, with all of your favorites one click away.*

The more sites we learn about, the greater our need to be able to organize and curate them. For some purposes, such as research, a robust tool with ample features to categorize and tag sites in a variety of ways is desired. For other purposes, such as for use as a dashboard, simplicity and ease of use may be the goal. Symbaloo is a perfect example of the latter school of thought. Their aim is to provide a concise layout of icons that provide one-click access to your favorite sites.

Symbaloo provides you a simple visual start page with tiles linking to your favorite web content.

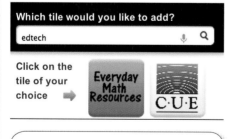

Search for terms to add sites to your webmix.

The interface within Symbaloo is called a webmix. Each webmix is comprised of sixty tiles laid out in a 10x6 grid. Click on any empty tile, and you'll have the option to populate it with a website. They have hundreds of websites saved in their database for you to choose from, or you can create your own by supplying a **URL** (universal or uniform reference locator) and customizing the look and feel of it. Select a blank square, specify what you want the tile to be, choose a design, and click submit. Repeat.

That's about it! While it may take a while to create a complete webmix, the majority of your time will be spent deciding what to include and arranging the tiles. The result is a dashboard intended to be used as a home page or launchpad. Load up the page, click on the site you want, and away you go.

http://edu.symbaloo.com/   class dashboard

symbalooEDU

Symbaloo is a classic example of the prototypical Web 2.0 tool that only does one thing but does it incredibly well. Like other simple tools though, the potential is unlocked when educators consider the many ways such a simple portal can be leveraged. The visual nature of the interface makes it an ideal way to share curated lists of websites/tools with others, particularly with people who may be intimidated by technology. A grid of tiles looks friendlier than a list of websites. While they may be identical from a functional perspective, Symbaloo's interface is much more inviting. It can be an ideal way to introduce colleagues to new technologies that may be of interest to them in a simple, nonthreatening way.

It has also become a favorite among elementary teachers who want to provide a launching point for student explorations. By creating webmixes for a variety of different topics, students are able to select a subject and be provided with a starter set of recommended sites to explore.

The big, bold tiles make it an ideal dashboard for using across multiple platforms. Like many web tools, it is browser and OS agnostic. The web interface is an elegant platform for accessing favorites on mobile devices. They have developed apps for both iOS and Android that provide a consistent experience with the web interface. Webmixes are a fantastic solution for educators who want to create launchpads that can be accessed by students regardless of their device or platform. An added bonus is that the large, colorful tiles are reminiscent of the way apps are laid out on mobile devices, making the experience feel familiar and intuitive.

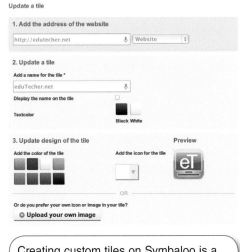

Creating custom tiles on Symbaloo is a piece of cake. Select the options you want, and you'll be all set.

There are some subtle features that are available to user created webmixes. When setting up a tile, users can specify if the site they are linking to is a news feed (RSS), radio station, or media that can be **embedded**. If a site is

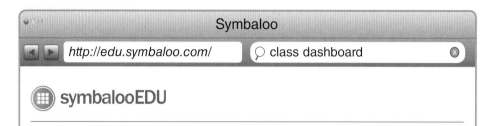

marked as a news feed, clicking on it will display a list of recent posts. Radio stations will provide a streaming audio interface, and embedded media (such as YouTube videos) will display the video without leaving the webmix itself.

There is an EDU portal for Symbaloo, but it does not provide too many benefits for educators. The free account is essentially identical to the traditional user accounts. For a yearly fee, educators get to customize their URL, create up to fifty student accounts, and tailor the branding of their webmixes slightly more. With a larger investment, intended for school or district purchases, users have additional branding options and access to analytics.

Classroom Idea—Mix Up Your Centers

Symbaloo makes an ideal launchpad for classroom computers during center time. Create several webmixes featuring content you are currently studying. For example, you might create a webmix devoted to phonics games, another featuring math songs, and a third focusing on science videos. Students who sit down during center time will have a variety of choices that all focus specifically on their current studies. Even better, a link to the webmixes can be sent home to parents, allowing them to use it to reinforce student learning.

Kick It Up a Notch—Energize Student Research

Add the Symbaloo **bookmarklet** to computers in the lab and provide the same username and password to all students. During lab time, have the students think about alternative energy sources. Discuss a few ideas and why it is important to learn about them. Then challenge them to find new sources for alternative energy and green living. As they find sites, videos, and articles worth saving, have them save it to a class webmix. When the mix begins to fill up, encourage the students consider how tiles could be grouped and split the set into several webmixes. After they have each found a few, students can explore each other's contributions to learn more about other new sources of energy.

http://edu.symbaloo.com/

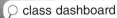 class dashboard ⊗

  symbalooEDU

Tweet Tweet: What Fellow Educators Are Saying

Symbaloo is set as our home pages on the computers, and the app is set on the iPads and iTouches. Being visual, all of the students K–12 find success with locating important resources. The webmixes we have created are also so easy to share with parents and others to use outside of school . . . keeping our students constantly connected to what they need.

Shannon Miller (@shannonmmiller)

Creating a Symbaloo page for my class has been a life saver. The colored tiles and icons and customizable look are perfect for making access to websites quick and easy for my younger elementary students.

Mary Beth Hertz (@mbteach)

Symbaloo has made it a snap for me to share accessible sites for my 2nd graders to access when they are using the classroom computers. Using visual icons that children recognize has allowed me to offer more of a 'choice' when they are exploring.

Cheryl Lykowski (@CLykowski)

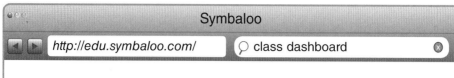

http://edu.symbaloo.com/   ⌕ class dashboard ⊗

Quick Tip: Create a visual playlist of educational songs. #Kinderchat has some wonderful examples of these. In Symbaloo, do a webmix search for Kinderchat to see them.

Click "add new tile," and paste the URL to a song on YouTube.

Organize songs by theme, and share the webmix with your students.

🎞 **See Symbaloo in Action**

 Research, Share, Collaborate

Social bookmarking was not only at the forefront of the Web 2.0 revolution; it has the distinction of introducing two concepts that have become critical to the way we interact with media today. The idea of sharing publicly the personal things that one is bookmarking may seem like a strange activity. However, once a critical mass of people began doing so, insights into what was noteworthy and significant to society could be gleaned based solely on what individuals were choosing to save. Rather than relying on experts to determine what was important and worth knowing, significance was based on individual activity bubbling up. This may seem like a minor change, but it was the precursor to such popular features as "Likes," +1s, and the simple thumbs-up.

The second distinction brought about by the social bookmarking movement was that it proved the value of folksonomies as a means of classifying information. While taxonomies rely on a fixed structure for organizing information, folksonomies (aka tagging) rely on the individual to add keywords that are meaningful to themselves. While the specific tags applied to a piece of information, such as a bookmark, may vary wildly between two individuals, as the number of people tagging it increases, the commonalities between their keywords become apparent. For example, while person A may tag a photo *poodle* and person B may tag it *canine,* there is a good chance that both of them, along with persons C, D, and E, all tag it with the keyword *dog.* In this way, the more people there are that participate in tagging a piece of information, the better the chance that consensus will occur, leading to a valid, relevant method of classifying information.

There were several sites that popularized social bookmarking—some that are still around (Delicious) and others that have since shut their doors (Furl). However, Diigo is one of the only sites that has not only managed to retain its popularity but has been consistent in its development efforts, pushing out new releases, plugins, apps, and more. From the beginning, it was popular among educators because of its robust feature set, including such academic options as highlighting, commenting, and also adding notes to the content being bookmarked. It is the sharing and networking features that have made it incredibly sticky, providing immense value even to those users that don't spend significant time bookmarking items.

diigo

Diigo is a site that requires some work on the part of the user before they will receive much reward from it. When you first sign in, your library will be empty, you won't be connected to anyone, and it may seem a bit confusing regarding what you are supposed to do. Think of it like a word processor. When you first open it up, all you'll see is a blank page. It's up to you to determine how you'll fill it.

The primary purpose of Diigo is to serve as a place to store your bookmarks (favorites) online. Many of us use several computers throughout the course of the day, as well as other devices such as smartphones or tablets. Diigo provides a central repository for your bookmarks so you can get access to them anywhere. You add bookmarks to the site in a variety of ways. The site recommends that you install a browser toolbar, which will provide you the most robust experience. If you are unable to install software on your computer, you can add their bookmarklet, the "diigolet," to your browser's favorites bar. Once you have done one of these two options, the next step is to find some things to bookmark.

Surf to a site that you believe is worth saving. Using the toolbar or diigolet, can highlight text on the page, add a note to it, or bookmark it to your Diigo account. By default, highlights and stickies are private, but if you have joined a group, you will be able to share those marks with the members of that community. As you bookmark a page, add a description and tags to help you organize your bookmarks. When you have just a few pages saved, it may not seem so critical to tag them. But as your collection grows, tags become a critical way to recover things that you may have saved months or even years ago.

Top 10 Tags	View All
education	1853
technology	943
web2.0	746
learning	732
tools	702
resources	431
classroom	398
science	351
teaching	305
web_2.0	292

Instead of putting sites into folders, tag them with keywords.

When you return to your Diigo library, you will see a chronological list of the things you have elected to save along with tags, notes, descriptions, and highlighted content. In the sidebar, a running list of all your

tags makes it simple to extract bookmarks based on a specific topic. The ability to return to this page from any computer makes bookmarking online a worthwhile activity, but this barely scratches the surface of the value that Diigo provides.

Users do have the option of saving any individual bookmark privately, but the vast majority choose to share what they are saving. Because of this, users can search the Diigo community and quickly determine the popularity of a given result. If an elementary math site has been bookmarked by 1,000 people, it likely has some relevancy and is worth exploring. As mentioned previously, people are also able to organize groups and share their discoveries with the members. In this way, a teacher can join in with like-minded colleagues and create an archive of sites that they feel are worth exploring, related specifically to their content area. Users can receive notification of submissions to that group via e-mail or simply by visiting the site. This can be incredibly useful, because it turns group members into a personal research team, sharing information and websites that you didn't even know were available. Instead of searching for new resources, group members bring them to you. In some sense, this sort of interactivity was a precursor to what many people now refer to as **personal learning networks** (PLNs).

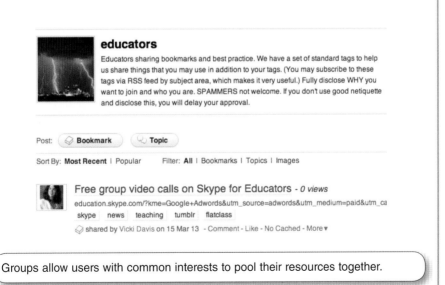

Groups allow users with common interests to pool their resources together.

There are many more features within Diigo that are worth exploring, as it has a great deal to offer students and educators. From mobile apps to browser-based extensions, Diigo has consistently proved that it can evolve with the rapidly shifting technological landscape. However, it's the core features that have made it so popular among educators. Some favorites include the caching of bookmarked sites (ensuring that users can get back to critical content even if the site is taken down later) and the ability to create curated lists of book-marks that can be shared with colleagues, students, or parents. Social book-marking via Diigo is a more in-depth process than many of the other sites shared in this book, but the rewards are well worth the effort.

Classroom Idea—Individual Papers, Group Research

When students are working on a research project, have them share with the class what topic they are studying. Students that will be researching similar topics should gather together and set up a private Diigo group (be sure to have them invite you as well). As they do their individual research, students will save their findings into the group pool along with any notes or highlighted passages. In this way, their research will be collaborative, but their actual work will be individualized. Being able to see who highlighted which passages will help ensure that no student relies too much on the work of their peers.

Kick It Up a Notch—Pitch in for Parents

Create a Diigo group, and invite colleagues who teach the same subject to join both at your school as well as within the district. As you find sites that you think would be beneficial for parents interested in providing support for their students at home, bookmark them into that group. If each member of the team adds resources as they discover them, parents will have access to a wealth of material that they know will be current and relevant, as it has been hand picked by teachers within that district.

diigo

Tweet Tweet: **What Fellow Educators Are Saying**

The ability to track student research at a glance and the ability for students to archive and access research from anywhere makes Diigo a great instructional and learning tool.

Ann Gardner (@virtualgardner)

A must have for all educators. Create a class group and tag and have students do the searching for you. Highlight and leave sticky notes on websites for your students. Diigo turns any website into an interactive conversation with your students.

Jeff Utecht (@jutecht)

Build your library of links, but don't forget to search other people's libraries—chances are, someone has spent more time bookmarking than you.

Jeff Layman (@Mrlaymanss)

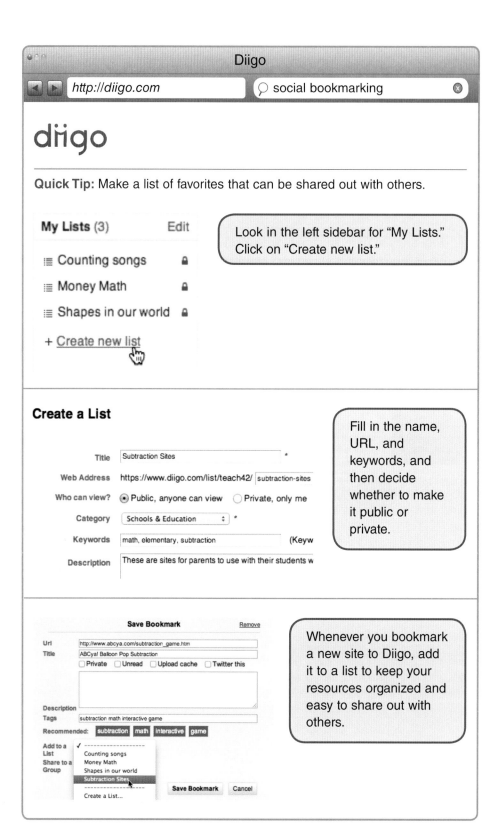

Diigo

http://diigo.com   ⌕ social bookmarking   ⊗

diigo

Quick Tip: Make a list of favorites that can be shared out with others.

My Lists (3)   Edit

≣ Counting songs   🔒

≣ Money Math   🔒

≣ Shapes in our world   🔒

+ Create new list

> Look in the left sidebar for "My Lists." Click on "Create new list."

Create a List

Title   Subtraction Sites   *

Web Address   https://www.diigo.com/list/teach42/ subtraction-sites

Who can view? ⦿ Public, anyone can view   ○ Private, only me

Category   Schools & Education   ⌄ *

Keywords   math, elementary, subtraction   (Keyw

Description   These are sites for parents to use with their students w

> Fill in the name, URL, and keywords, and then decide whether to make it public or private.

Save Bookmark   Remove

Url   http://www.abcya.com/subtraction_game.htm

Title   ABCya! Balloon Pop Subtraction

☐ Private ☐ Unread ☐ Upload cache ☐ Twitter this

Description

Tags   subtraction math interactive game

Recommended: subtraction math interactive game

Add to a   ✓ --------------------
List   Counting songs
Share to a   Money Math
Group   Shapes in our world
              Subtraction Sites
              --------------------   Save Bookmark   Cancel
              Create a List...

> Whenever you bookmark a new site to Diigo, add it to a list to keep your resources organized and easy to share out with others.

diigo

Quick Tip: Add educators to your network within Diigo to see what's popular right now.

56 people

Hacking the Classroom:
usergeneratededucation.wordpres:
designthinking   design   educat

> The number on the left of a bookmark in Diigo indicates how many other people have saved it. Click on it to see a list of those people.

41 people

22 Rules of Story Telling and Mobile Learning
www.educatorstechnology.com/...
storytelling   writing   via:packrat

Peggy George 191 followings **307** followers
Mac enthusiast, recently retired teacher educator at principal after 25 years, AzTEA Board member(Ariz and advocate for Web 2.0, Co-hosting weekly show
web2.0   education   technology   tools   blog
socialnetworking   learning

> Based on their tags and comments, choose a user you'd like to connect with and click their name.

191 followings, **307** followers

Follow Me!

Peggy George follows 191 people

> Browse through their saved resources. If they look valuable to you, click the "Follow Me!" link in the upper right.

Items from 211 People I follow

Global warming: More Americans believe 'big lie' | Sun Journa
Shared by Craig Cunningham, 1 save total
8 minutes ago · Preview · Comment · Like · Save

Whose Fault Is It Anyway??? | Small Bytes
Whose Fault Is It Anyway??? http://t.co/48m7wXRA #coetail
Shared by Jeff Utecht, 1 save total
12 minutes ago · Preview · Comment · Like · Save

Will · Interesting Disclaimer by Common Core Assessors
Interesting Disclaimer by Common Core Assessors
Shared by Will Richardson, 1 save total
about 1 hour ago · Preview · Comment · Like · Save

Technology Tools for 21st Century Learners v3.0
Shared by Tami Brass, 1 save total
about 1 hour ago · Preview · Comment · Like · Save

> From then on, when you click on "My Network," you will see recently added sites bookmarked by the people that you have followed.

See Diigo in Action

www.educlipper.net social resource community

 *Clip anything. Share everything.*

A note from the author:
Hello, Adam here. eduClipper is a tool very near and dear to my heart since I am both the founder and CEO.

Why did I create such a tool? That's easy. Finding and sharing educational resources on the web is something that I have spent countless hours doing for the past several years. I am a very visual learner, and I saw that visual bookmarking tools like Pinterest were appealing to a huge number of people as they helped to change the way people were sharing web content. eduClipper is a web tool that I developed that aims at changing the way educators curate and share information with their colleagues and students in the K–12 education space. And now, on with the details.

As you know, there are so many great digital resources available out there in the vast World Wide Web. There are web tools, such as the ones we've shared in this book, insightful articles, inspiring videos, and interactive websites that allow students to explore everything from ancient history to zoology. The amount of content is so vast that it can be hard to find quality resources that have been vetted by teachers or students in the same grade or subject area. And while there are many ways to collaborate with others online, sharing content and feedback is often limited to the people you have personally "friended."

eduClipper is a platform designed specifically for teachers and students that addresses these issues and allows you and your students to find, collect, and share web content quickly. It addresses problems that some educators face with respect to digital curation by allowing users to clip content from anywhere on the web, create auto-citations, and tag the content with labels aligned to K–12 areas of study. You can also choose whom to share the content with if you want to maintain stricter controls over privacy. While content can be kept private and only shared with users of your choice, the site is open by default, encouraging you to provide rich content for all to explore.

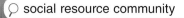 www.educlipper.net ⚲ social resource community

educlipper

In the introduction to this book, we mentioned that one feature to look for is whether the site plays nicely with other web tools and provides an exit strategy if you decide to look elsewhere. eduClipper provides both of these in spades. eduClipper lets users export the resources they have saved to other sites so that users' content is not locked down to one particular platform.

Teachers and students can register for free and use the tool independent of each other. But as an educator, you can create student accounts that allow you to monitor, moderate, and manage their content.

eduClipper was designed for the K–12 space, which is why teachers have so much control regarding how open or closed their students' networks are. Some content that is acceptable for an eighth grader may not be appropriate for a first grader. That is why elementary school students are unable to follow people outside of their class without teacher permission. Teachers have complete control over the features their students get access to.

Finding content on eduClipper is easy for educators. The default view highlights the most popular content on the site. However, if you teach third grade, you can personalize the experience to only show links that are targeted specifically for third grade teachers and students. Through the navigation bar, you can view the most popular links throughout the network, content from the users you follow, or your own content.

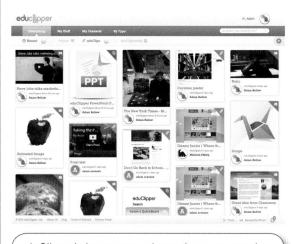

eduClipper's home page shows the most popular links that people have been sharing.

eduClipboards allow you to organize collections of eduClips. Users create a curated set of content for personal use or to share with others. It is a great way to pull together curricular resources for students or content collections to share among district teams.

www.educlipper.net   ○ social resource community   ⊗

educlipper

Each eduClipboard can be shared with individual users, groups of users, entire classes, or even posted to other popular social networks. Users can embed both eduClips and eduClipboards to personal blogs or school websites.

Create an eduClipboard with content that you like from the site, and organize it into categories that work for you and your students.

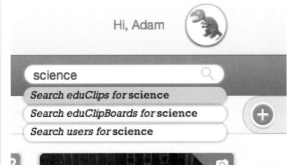

The eduClipper search feature makes it easy to find content related to a specific school-specific category.

There are a few ways to add content to the site. For easy eduClipping, you can install the "eduClip It" button in your browser. Once installed, surf as normal, and click it when you find content that you wish to save. The content can be an image, link, video, PDF, PPT, or just about any other type of media. You'll be prompted to title and tag the eduClip as well as to select which eduClipboard you want to add it to. Teachers and students (when allowed) can work collaboratively, contributing content to a common location. This is a great way for individuals to make contributions to class research projects, letting students collect and support each other's efforts.

eduClipper is aware that being a "good digital citizen" is really important. On many sites, it is easy to save information but difficult to cite it. That is why eduClipper integrated EasyBib functionality, which automatically adds appropriate citations and keeps track of who on the site was first to discover the item.

educlipper

Students can use the site to collect links with their fellow students, save items for their own reference, and share resources that they find with their teacher. However, one of the features that really sets eduClipper apart is that students can use the content they save to create a personal **digital portfolio**. As more schools move toward holistic assessment methods, capturing students' tangible projects as well as their digital work is increasingly important to showcase. Content that students create elsewhere on the web can easily be eduClipped into a portfolio.

eduClipper is a deceptively simple site. While it can take minutes to jump in and start using it to curate content, the number of educator-friendly features that it offers is truly astounding. It was created by an educator for fellow educators and students, so it has taken into account little details that other sites may not have considered.

No Cell Phones in Class...
eduClipped 11 days ago
Mildred Phillip

Hover over an eduClip to see all the options you have to share it.

Classroom Idea—Creating eduExperts

Many schools have study-buddy programs that pair older and younger learners together so that the older students can act as mentors to the younger students. You can take this idea to the next level on eduClipper. Allow the students in your class to pick the subject that they are interested or expert in and give them the challenge to create a clipboard with the best resources available on that subject. Each of the eduClipboards can be compiled into a class board that acts as a textbook supplement or even digital replacement. The student created clipboards will serve as a great reference for all their classmates as well as other students and teachers on the site looking for support content in those areas.

www.educlipper.net   ○ social resource community   ⊗

educ‖ipper

Kick It Up a Notch—Portfolios for Students to Share

eduClipper is a great tool for creating student digital portfolios. Even beyond that, it is also a tool that teachers can use to start expanding the way a student is assessed when it comes time for annual or quarterly report cards. Allowing students to showcase their best work as it pertains to your class is a great way to find out about the students' strengths as well as where they need support. You can easily set up projects through the teacher dashboard and let students submit their work through the site for your assessments, which can be left as either voice or written messages. Using eduClipper's digital portfolio tools, you can turn the traditional share-session into a collaborative web activity that allows students from other classes to weigh in and provide feedback, giving students the chance to learn from each other.

www.educlipper.net   ○ social resource community

 educlipper

Tweet Tweet: What Fellow Educators Are Saying

Getting content in front of learners at the point in time they need it will ensure passion-based independent learning trajectories are a reality.

Adam Aronson (@adam_aronson)

Educators are desperate to organize the hundreds of websites and tools that are available on the web, and before eduClipper, there was no easy way to do that.

James Sanders (@jamestsanders)

Why do I love eduClipper? Because it's ALL education ALL the time! AWESOME!

Krissy Venosdale (@ktvee)

www.educlipper.net   🔍 social resource community   ⊗

edu[lipper

Quick Tip: Create a collaborative eduClipboard, and allow students to all curate resources together on the same board.

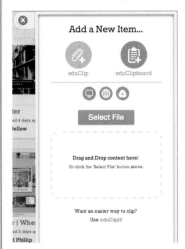

Click on the Add Content "+" on the left side of the navigation bar. Select "Board," and click on the option to create a collaborative clipboard.

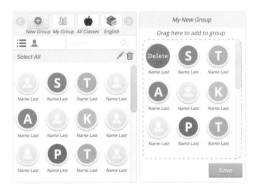

When you're creating the Collaborative Board, you can select a group of students to invite to the board or create a new group of students. Simply drag and drop their avatars to the box on the right that says "add recipients here . . ."

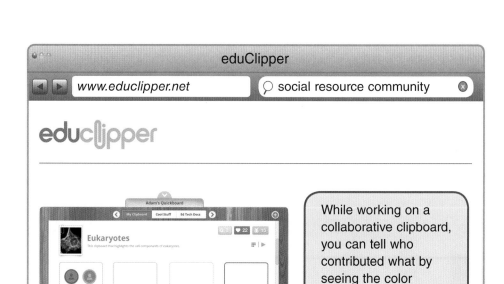

While working on a collaborative clipboard, you can tell who contributed what by seeing the color highlight around their profile picture, and the same color will be the border of the content that they have eduClipped.

See eduClipper in Action

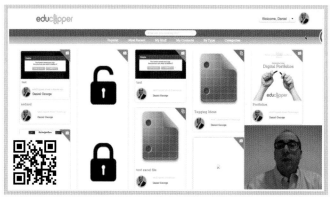

Visit the online community at www.untanglingthewebcommunity.com.

2

ARTISTIC TOOLS

Unleash Your Creative Side

Steve Jobs, Apple's late cofounder, famously said, "Technology alone is not enough—it's technology married with liberal arts, married with the humanities, that yields us the result that makes our heart sing." He was absolutely right.

For the past several years (arguably for much longer than that), schools have been making difficult decisions when it comes to arts education. Drama, dance, music, and traditional art programs of all kinds have been marginalized and in some cases cut entirely from schools in order to provide what is seen as the "essentials." The arts are extremely important to creating a well-rounded person, and infusing them in all aspects of curriculum will yield a more creative, engaged, and capable student.

Technology does not replace traditional arts education but can enhance learning experiences by helping students engage in content, create new understandings, and publish work with the class or world at large.

Thinking back to the earliest classroom machines, you are likely to remember such titles as Broderbund's Print Shop. Many of us remember the banners that would slowly be churned out on a dot matrix printer—page by page by page. Back then, that program, which is still around today, allowed students and educators to create cards, banners, and other printed works that could work to support the classroom experience. Another popular piece of software is KidPix, a creative art studio that allows students to create artwork using digital tools like stamps, pens, markers, and text. These software titles are great examples of the kinds of products that the web-based counterparts we will be exploring are akin to. They are fairly straightforward and simple to use on one level but can create elaborate demonstrations of learning.

This chapter explores tools that allow students to manipulate graphics, author original songs, and collaborate on video projects that can be as creative and unique as each individual student. The ability to create truly remarkable works of art that express a student's understanding has evolved with modern technology. Free web-based tools now rival expensive software that schools were allocating thousands of dollars to a few years ago.

Enjoy exploring these tools that give you the paint, microphone, and special effects to empower your students' ideas.

Big Huge Labs

www.bighugelabs.com/education.php   photo projects

Helping you do cool stuff with your photos.

Big Huge Labs is a treasure trove of simple tools that revolve around images. This site, which has been "helping you do cool stuff with your photos since 2005," is chock-full of more than thirty short activities to help kick off, enhance, and creatively express their understanding of a study topic. To be honest, there are some that are just plain fun, too.

People have been editing photos and images for use in class projects almost as long as computers have been around. Do you get nostalgic thinking about using Print Shop to create posters and banners with clip art images? Or perhaps you remember editing and drawing with simple tools like Microsoft Paint or KidPix. Big Huge Labs lets educators combine template-based image editing with their own creative project ideas.

The Big Huge Labs home page easily links to all the great creative projects the site has to offer.

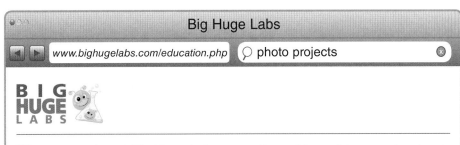

When you arrive at Big Huge Labs, you will want to register as a teacher in order to remove the ads on the site and be able to create student accounts. Registration is not required, but signing up with a valid e-mail and sending proof that you're an educator is well worth it. Student account creation is fairly simple and can be accomplished by entering names manually or by importing a spreadsheet with their information. There are even handouts with auto-generated student IDs that you can print and distribute.

Big Huge Labs is all about creatively expressing ideas through images. The projects, while technically simple (upload, add text, send/save/print), can be an exciting alternative assessment for students. Every project on the site can be completed in less than thirty minutes.

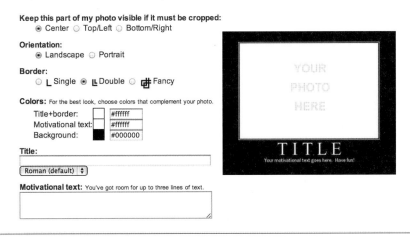

All it takes to create a cool motivational poster is to follow the simple prompts.

Big Huge Labs serves as a creative studio with helpful resources to guide users through the process. Students can upload photos to a calendar, add descriptive text on important dates, and print it out. Map Maker lets your students highlight different geographic areas around the world with different colors. While intended to show where in the world one has been or wants to visit, this is a perfect way to identify locations in a story or to document countries touched by a particular natural disaster. The user customizes the particular colors on the map, so they can define how the information is displayed. The result can be printed or embedded into a webpage.

www.bighugelabs.com/education.php | ○ photo projects ⊗

Classroom Idea—Motivated by Vocabulary

One of the most popular features on Big Huge Labs is the motivational posters it can generate. You've seen those, right? The picture of a cat hanging from a tree surrounded by big black borders with the text "Hang in there" along the bottom? They can be a perfect way to reinforce vocabulary terms. The next time you give out a vocabulary assignment, have the students take one word and create a poster using the Big Huge Labs motivational poster tool. Associating it with an image and/or tagline is a simple way for them to demonstrate concrete understanding. Students can use a digital camera to provide their own image or find an image online to use. Once the posters are created, you can print them out and decorate the class. It is a great way for them to learn the meanings of new words while creating fun decor for your room.

Motivational posters are easy to create and can be a fun way to add inspiration and humor to the classroom.

Kick It Up a Notch—Collectible Learning

Trading cards can combine the creative aspects of the site with your current topic of study. For example, ask the students to create a set of cards featuring the entire cast of a Shakespearean play. Students can select a title, tagline, description, and image for each character, along with minor details such as icons and cost. Print them out on card stock, cut them out, and let the students trade with each other. These activities can be challenging to do but will leave students with flash cards that are more than learning tools ... they're collectibles!

BIG HUGE LABS

Tweet Tweet: What Fellow Educators Are Saying

My students make magazine posters of themselves in the future using the tools here. Lots of fun, cool things to do.

Vicki Davis (@coolcatteacher)

Images are a gateway to language and writing, as well as a connection to topics and concepts. They allow you to stimulate discussion and build a common vocabulary.

Adina Sullivan (@adinasullivan)

I use Big Huge Labs with my 5th grade when we do our "Survivor MD" body system research project. They make their "doctor" ID badges to wear during project—they are doctors 'stranded' on an island that have to compete in various body system-related tasks! They LOVE doing this. You can see an example here (scroll down to bottom of page).

Karen Kliegman (@kkliegman)

I had my tech club make badges for themselves (middle schoolers). I thought they could care less about them, until the next year started and they wore them to our first meeting. Now it's a tradition! One mom even said her 8th grader wears it when he helps her on the computer at home! Never underestimate the power of a badge or a middle schooler!

Sheila Adams (@sheila_a)

www.bighugelabs.com/education.php   ○ photo projects   ⊗

Quick Tip: Make a simple matching game using images from your current unit.

Mosaic Maker

Make a mosaic from a photoset, favorites, tags, or individual digital photographs or images. It's a whole world of creative photo possibilities.

Select Mosaic Maker, and create a grid with an even number of squares.

Click "Choose photo" below (or one of the images

Upload pairs of images.

1.   Or enter URL:

http://flickr.com/pho

2.   Or enter URL:

http://flickr.com/pho

Print out your mosaic, and cut out the images to create the game.

See Big Huge Labs in Action

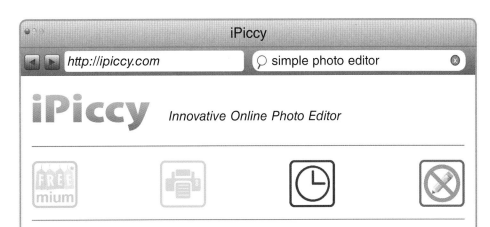

Most educators have fairly basic photo editing needs. We crop, we resize, we need to get rid of a red eye or two. Occasionally we may want to brighten a photo or change it from color to black and white. More often than not, educators would gladly trade a bloated, full-featured photo editing application for a lightweight one that fulfills 95 percent of their needs, works on every computer they own, and is completely free. And that's where iPiccy shines.

Because it's web-based, iPiccy will work regardless of your operating system or browser. It loads incredibly quickly and handles most people's photo editing needs. In addition to the basics mentioned previously, it also provides easy interfaces to adjust exposure, colors, levels, curves, and other more sophisticated tweaks. The beauty of iPiccy, though, is that it does it through an intuitive interface that even novices will feel comfortable exploring. With every tool you choose, you see a preview of the changes you are making and always have the chance to cancel or undo should you change your mind.

If you're feeling creative, iPiccy provides a wide variety of filters to customize your photos. As with the other tweaks, the same simple interface can be used to turn your photo into a comic, a pencil drawing, a wanted poster, or one of many color options. There are an incredible number to choose from, and they rotate the options

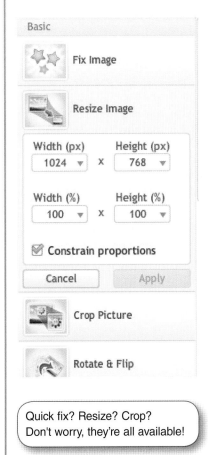

iPiccy

fairly regularly. There are ample options for touching up digital photos, allowing users to remove blemishes and wrinkles, apply a tan, change eye colors, or to shed a few pounds with the "Thinify" tool.

What's incredible about iPiccy is that the more time you spend with it, the more you realize that it actually has an impressive number of features that you would normally expect to only find in expensive photo editing programs. However, not only are they available for free but they're also simplified enough to make them accessible to the average user. Some of these features include an interface for layering photos, adding vector masks, and even using a clone tool for sophisticated touch-up jobs. There is also a collage interface that enables users to combine multiple photos into creative layouts as quickly and easily as the rest of the site. When aggregated together, this simple little photo editor is actually incredibly robust.

While it does require **Flash** to run, there is no registration required. In fact, there isn't even the option of registering if you wanted to! Enabling local storage allows you to save photos within the site for future use. After editing a photo, you can download it as a **JPEG** (or JPG) or **PNG** (portable network graphics) file, share a link to it via URL, or save it to Flickr. There may not be many options for importing photos in or exporting them to other sites, but the features and interface more than make up for this deficiency. Not only is it a powerful editor, but it is ideal for educational use.

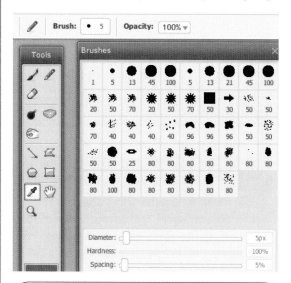

A hidden gem within iPiccy is the drawing tool. It's no Illustrator, but it gets the job done!

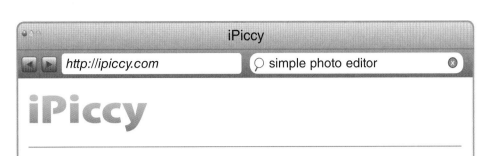

Classroom Idea—Postcards From the Past

During the Age of Discovery, the explorers didn't have access to blogs, **tweets,** or e-mails. But they did employ the use of traditional mail to communicate with people back home. Have students document the voyages of these brave individuals through a series of faux postcards created within iPiccy. For every step along their journey, have the students identify a primary image, format it in the shape of a postcard, and then add text documenting what the students think the explorers would choose to share with their friends and families back home.

Upload your photos, import them from a link or Flickr, or take a new photo using your webcam.

Kick It Up a Notch—Getting Your Bob Ross On . . .

Considering that iPiccy is a photo editor, one might think that there aren't many advanced uses. The real trick to taking a site like iPiccy to the next level is to combine it with the other sites, like the ones in this book. For example, everybody loves Wordle, but after a while, all Wordles tend to look rather similar. However, by saving the **word cloud** as an image and then importing it into iPiccy, educators can add a large degree of customization to it. Simple things like adding a frame give it a new look and feel and using custom filters can apply a style that makes something traditional look impressively fresh. But the real fun begins when you begin adding stickers, callouts, and drawings to further accentuate the theme the word cloud itself. For example, if the word cloud is about seasons, add stickers related to weather and seasonal activities. Then use the drawing tools to highlight the key words in the cloud. Add a frame or matte to it and you have created a Wordle unlike any other!

http://ipiccy.com | simple photo editor

iPiccy

Tweet Tweet: What Fellow Educators Are Saying

You simply click the Start Editing button to begin. Students and teachers can easily use this free site to retouch, fix, and embellish images they might use on a website or in a project.

Tony Vincent (@tonyvincent)

If you wish to add a bit of "ohh ahhh" to your photos then iPiccy is your site. It is a user-friendly—NO DOWNLOAD REQUIRED—photo editing tool that can be utilized by students (and teachers) of all comfort levels. If you just want to add an arrow to a screen shot—you can do so. If you wish to create layers, bevels, gradients, effects, and more—you can do that as well. Quick and easy upload to many social media locations.

Jennifer Wagner (@jenwagner)

What makes iPiccy stand out is its accessibility. This rich featured photo editing tool requires no download or log in making it a great tool to use with students and teachers alike. The tool allows for a lot of creativity and can help you make good pictures great.

Martha Thornburgh (@roswellsgirl)

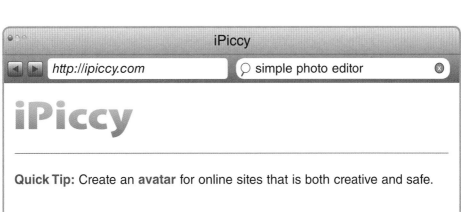

iPiccy

Quick Tip: Create an **avatar** for online sites that is both creative and safe.

Use a webcam to get a basic photo of you or your student.

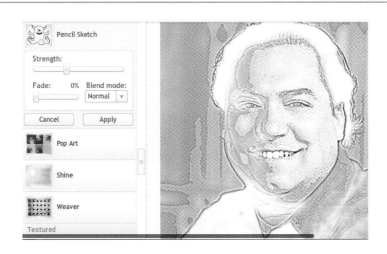

Use the many filters and effects available to add individual touches and to make it safe to use on social networks.

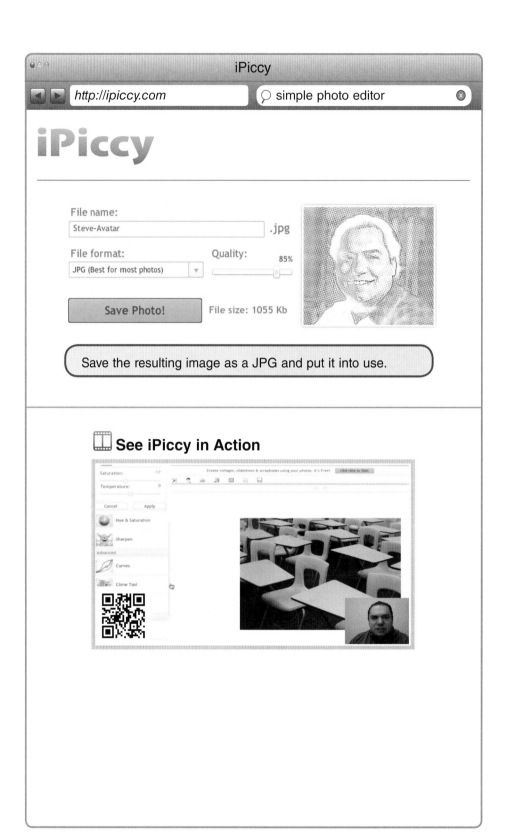

http://sumopaint.com   ○ advanced image editing   ⊗

Free edition   *Unleash your creativity!*

Sumo Paint is an amazingly full-featured drawing application. It is hands down one of the most powerful web-based art tools to date. At a glance, Sumo Paint is remarkably similar to the ever-popular software titles from Adobe, an extraordinary mash-up of both Photoshop and Illustrator. Beyond the obvious benefits of being web-based and platform independent, it has both a free version as well as premium features available at a fraction of the cost of the software that inspired it.

Look familiar? If you're a Photoshop user, it does.

So what does Sumo Paint do? It is really all about what it enables you and your students to do. You can upload a previously created image and use Sumo Paint to crop, resize, and perform basic editing. But that is not where the tool shines. Where you get the most bang for your buck is in the plethora of brushes and customizable drawing tools to choose from. Among the options

are chalk, oil, airbrush, and even symbols (like a smiley face). You can alter the colors, background, and shadows; adjust lighting effects; or convert the entire image to a geometric shape. The possibilities are as endless as the imagination of the user, and it can be used equally effectively as a photo editor or as a drawing tool.

Advanced users of Photoshop (and the other similar products) may be wondering if Sumo Paint is as robust as its software-based counterparts. They will be pleasantly surprised to find features like layers are not only present but are implemented in a virtually identical manner. Layers give you the ability to combine multiple images on the same canvas, combining them visually without actually merging them together. You can manipulate the transparency of a layer or adjust the order of the layers so that when they are combined with shadow effects, it's easy to create the feeling of depth.

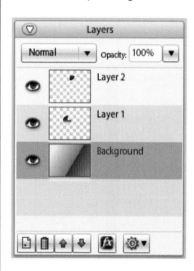

While there is an online art gallery for users of Sumo Paint to showcase their work, this can also be problematic at some grade levels. A public gallery can be a powerful way to share, but because it is not moderated, it may contain material that could be considered objectionable to students. This is certainly an aspect of the site that should be carefully considered by the teacher to determine if it is enough of a concern to avoid using it.

Layers, brushes, and filters are all available to students who are ready to take graphic design to the next level.

Sumo Paint does have a free registration process that provides benefits such as saving to the **Cloud,** but this is completely optional. Users can just visit the site and begin creating. As we have cautioned elsewhere, an important feature to look for is the ability to save your creations outside of the web tool itself. Sumo Paint does indeed give the user multiple

ways to save their work and store their creations both onsite (if registered) and locally on their own computer.

Sumo Paint is available in app form for Chrome, Edmodo, and iOS.

Classroom Idea—21st-Century Cave Drawings

Using art to tell a story is an idea that hearkens back to the days of cave dwellers. But being able to freely publish and share stories with anyone in the world is a relatively new phenomenon. A great project that will allow your students to express themselves creatively is group storytelling. As a class, create an idea for a story. This can be typed up in a collaborative Google Doc or just shared on the chalkboard. Ask students to illustrate each event from the story in Sumo Paint. Start with volunteers first and assign the remainder. Students will create a single image or series of images for the event and save them. Collect the images and arrange them in sequence to illustrate the story. To make it a true slideshow, import the photos into a site like Slideshare or Voicethread.

Bonus points: Have your students incorporate the current week's vocabulary words in the story!

Kick It Up a Notch—Get Your Geometry in Shape

One of the hidden gems (or at least underused) is the amazing shape tools that Sumo Paint has. These preset tools allow students to create and manipulate shapes, both 2D and 3D. This takes a tool that is commonly thought of as a tool for the arts and makes it incredibly relevant to math classes. When exploring fractions, use the pie tool to help visualize the difference between one-eighth and one-fourth. Draw a wedge on the screen, and let students try to guess what fraction it is. Then allow students to create their own fraction-inspired artwork. After they complete their project, have the students use the text tool to label each individual pie piece with the correct fraction.

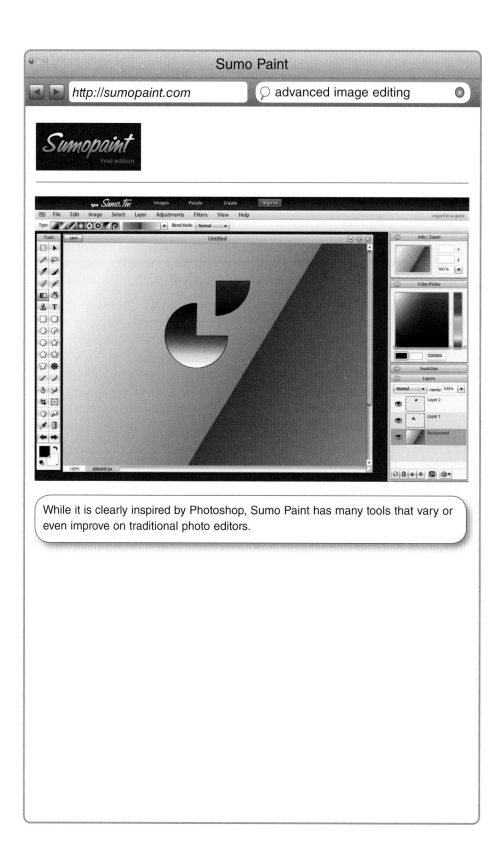

While it is clearly inspired by Photoshop, Sumo Paint has many tools that vary or even improve on traditional photo editors.

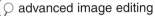 advanced image editing

Tweet Tweet: **What Fellow Educators Are Saying**

Sumo Paint is a free alternative to expensive creativity suites like Photoshop. The set of tools is just big enough to edit photos and create sharp graphics without it being too much to learn. The fact that it is Cloud-based really helps with the school-to-home work piece. Students can access their creations from any computer, not just the one they get to use during lab time.

Andy Losik (@mrlosik)

Sumo Paint has many of the features of Photoshop without any downloads or cost. The layers feature allows students to create complex artwork and graphic designs.

Selena Ward (@thetechtiger)

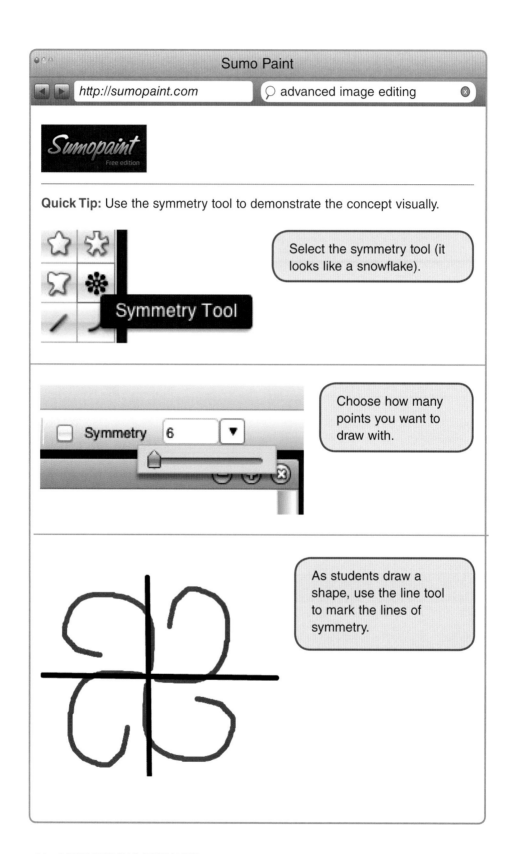

Sumo Paint

http://sumopaint.com   advanced image editing

Sumopaint
Free edition

Quick Tip: Use the symmetry tool to demonstrate the concept visually.

Select the symmetry tool (it looks like a snowflake).

Symmetry Tool

Choose how many points you want to draw with.

Symmetry   6

As students draw a shape, use the line tool to mark the lines of symmetry.

 *Make your music.*

In ancient days, music was employed to help people remember oral histories and folktales. It is a powerful medium for locking information in through mnemonic triggers. Look back on your own education, and you'll likely recall some of the first experiences you had in the classroom revolving around music. Can you recite the alphabet without falling into the cadence associated with the song? Nearly everyone has a penchant for music, and while styles and tastes vary, it is a commonality we all enjoy. However, after grade school music is often treated as an elective and is underutilized in classrooms.

It hasn't always been easy to create digital music. Until recently, one would need expensive hardware, cables, and microphones in order to record a complete song. Recently this has begun to change. Software-based tools such as GarageBand and Songsmith have made music creation much more accessible to the average user. However, there are few web-based alternatives that are notable enough to be considered for general educational use. uJam is one of the few that not only makes it easy to create, edit, and remix music but opens up the genre to every classroom and grade level.

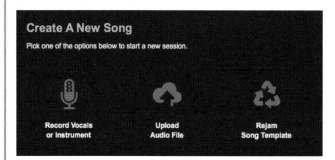

Choose to record from your microphone, upload a song you already have, or remix someone else's songs.

There are two distinct versions of the uJam platform. UJAM Studio allows users to become both a performer and producer, creating a song and mixing to their liking. It can also be used to remix songs created by other users. Remixing a song is a great way for your students to concentrate on writing lyrics and editing the content of the song while still having a great outcome. It gives students a starting point from which to build on. The site also features Jam-a-Gram, an app for creating an audio greeting. While this can be a fun activity, the studio is most relevant for use in an educational setting.

What sets uJam apart from some of the other tools out there is that students don't need to know anything about music in order to make an awesome sounding song. Users can speak, sing, or even hum a tune into the tool. It will determine what key they were in and create a chord structure around it. Using the basic interface, you can select a style of music to use in the background, and uJam will turn your recording into a complete song. It doesn't matter what key you sang in, or even if you were in a key at all. uJam will analyze your voice and harmonize with it.

For those desiring a more advanced experience, uJam also provides the ability to customize the specific instruments that will be used, the chord progression, or even the structure of specific chords within the song. Basic users can change the song from blues to rap with a single click while musicians can spend hours tweaking projects to match the exact sound they are looking for.

Your students can use the computer's built-in microphone to record their audio.

The ease of use makes it incredibly accessible to even those without a large degree of musical talent. So long as the user can stay on the beat (a metronome is provided while recording), the songs that uJam creates are surprisingly pleasing to the ear. This makes it an ideal means for adding music to poetry or to create a mnemonic device for remembering a data set (prime numbers, state capitals, etc.). Creating a

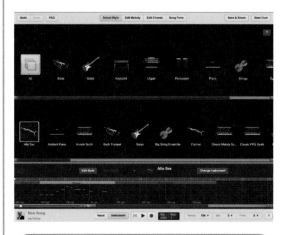

After you record your song, you can change the pitch and even convert the audio to sound like other instruments.

song not only personalizes the experience but makes it all the more memorable.

While you can save songs within the site in order to edit them at a later time, the exact number is based on your activities. Registering for the site allows you to save a single song while completing your profile and inviting friends bumps that number up to as high as seven. Every creation can be downloaded to your computer as an mp3, playable on all modern music devices.

Classroom Idea—Cue the Opening Music

Podcasting has become a popular way for students to share classroom experiences. Finding educationally appropriate and copyright friendly music to include can be quite a challenge. Have the students create a theme song for the class that will be used as the opener and closer for the class podcast. This can easily be done as a group project and is a great way to get more students involved in the podcasting experience. Have one group create the lyrics. So long as they adhere to a basic rhythm and rhyme scheme, they will work fine for this purpose. Have another student (or group of students) come up with a basic melody and sing it into uJam. Then have a third use the studio to create a mix to use in the podcast.

Bonus points: If other students have a different vision for what the song should sound like, let them create their own remix of it! Every show could feature a new remix of the podcast theme.

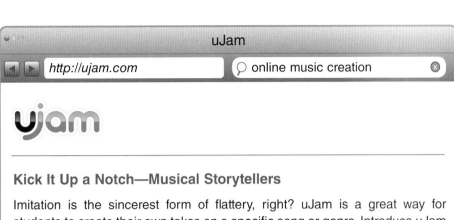

Kick It Up a Notch—Musical Storytellers

Imitation is the sincerest form of flattery, right? uJam is a great way for students to create their own takes on a specific song or genre. Introduce uJam to students, and give them time to explore. Play a popular song for them, such as Billy Joel's "We Didn't Start the Fire." Break down the song as a class, and discuss the historical events that were documented within the song. Next, have each student create his or her own song that summarizes a historical period of time. They will need to research that period, identify key events that will need to be included, and determine how they will include them as lyrics. Provide a quiet space for students to go record their lyrics—after which they can return to the lab to do the mixing. When the students have completed their projects, allow them to present their songs to the class and explain the choices they made in creating it.

Tweet Tweet: What Fellow Educators Are Saying

Record your voice; mix with funk or Latin or another track; save online or download as MP3. Best part? They keep making it better!

Rushton Hurley (@rushtonh)

Their sound editor (think GarageBand but web-based) is super easy to use with tracks and instruments recorded by real musicians. Their algorithms turn my spoken word into lyrical masterpieces.

Matt Monjan (@monjan)

uJam

http://ujam.com   🔍 online music creation   ⊗

Quick Tip: If you want to get even more hands on, you can customize even the tiniest details in your instrumental track.

After selecting a musical genre, click on "Edit Style."

Select the specific instruments that you want to include in your song.

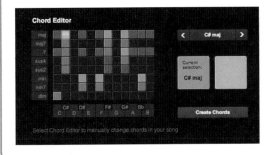

If you really want to get granular, click on "Edit Chords," and modify them till you get the exact sound you're looking for.

WeVideo

www.wevideo.com — video editor

weVIDEO *Collaborative Online Video Editor in the Cloud*

For over 100 years, video has been one of the most dynamic mediums in which a story can be told. Creating video has been challenging in a school setting because of several factors. Most notably, desktop editing software that can only make use of video saved locally on the hard drive limits the creative process to the times that a student has access to that specific machine. In the past, the Cloud has offered few solutions for video editing. WeVideo is a tool that allows users to upload video to the web and edit it online in a rich editor that rivals many of the major desktop software tools that classrooms have traditionally used. The advantage to being web-based is that users can access their files anywhere they can get online. Additionally, it is not operating system dependent. No longer would a student need to wait to get time on one specific classroom machine—their creative process can extend well beyond the walls of the school day.

WeVideo offers all the functionality of your desktop editors . . . but it's all in the Cloud.

www.wevideo.com   video editor

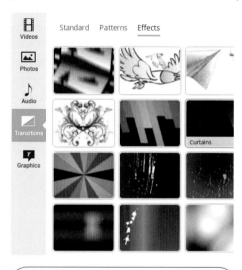

Spice up your videos with tons of digital effects that you can drag and drop onto your video timeline.

WeVideo offers a real-time video editor. There is no rendering, and all the editing and effects are added and seen on the fly. The interface is simple to use and offers familiar drag and drop functionality similar to desktop titles like Windows Movie Maker and iMovie.

WeVideo improved upon the concept of editing on the web by making the process collaborative. Students can share projects and work with one another to complete it. This comes in very handy for group projects, as students from the same class can share their library of footage with each other. This allows all students in the group to create their own mix of the project. WeVideo provides a good number of transitions between clips as well as video filters and effects to spice up the production. There are also dozens of royalty free songs and sound effects that can be used in your projects. Images and additional music can be uploaded, but it is the responsibility of the users to respect copyright laws.

WeVideo has also built in some incredible features that make use of other technologies that schools may be using such as Google Drive, Dropbox, and Box.net. This allows the video files to be synced, saved, and shared from a Cloud-based storage accounts, adding another layer of security and increasing storage capacity.

WeVideo provides basic, intermediate, and advanced versions of their editor, allowing users to select the level of sophistication they are most comfortable with. If you're using the simple editor and realize you have more complex needs, you can switch versions at any time. They have also released an Android

WeVideo

www.wevideo.com | video editor

wevideo

Set to private

Publish now

Set resolution — 480p

Publish to — WeVideo

wevideo
WeVideo
Connected

You Tube
YouTube
Connected

vimeo
Vimeo
Not connected

Dropbox

Google Drive

Manage accounts

When your video is done, you can choose a wide range of ways to share or export the content.

editor (only for select devices) and an iOS uploader. The iOS app allows users to record footage via their device and upload it straight into their project for editing through the web interface.

With the free plan, your storage is limited and you are provided a basic amount of export minutes per month. Their premium education subscription plans are fairly reasonable and allow users increased storage and export time as well as the ability to save videos in HD without the WeVideo watermark.

Classroom Idea—And . . . Action!

Have students examine a period in history and create a short skit that they film, edit, and debut for their class. One area where video can be particularly effective is in language arts. Have students reenact a scene from one of the books or plays that they have read. They can alternatively create a sequel, prequel, or a scene that is only inferred by the author. Making videos part of your classroom isn't complicated. Always start with the writing. Have students storyboard out the concept for their video and turn that concept into a script, complete with descriptive direction for the characters. Allow the students to decide how to cast the video. Record your footage using mobile cameras or digital video recorders and upload it to WeVideo. Divide the project into scenes and assign groups of students to begin editing. Bring it all together, and export it as one complete video.

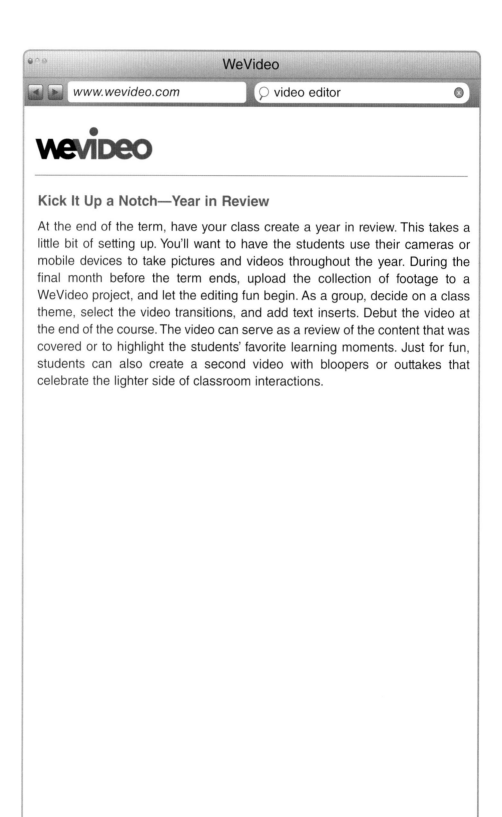

WeVideo

www.wevideo.com

video editor

wevideo

Kick It Up a Notch—Year in Review

At the end of the term, have your class create a year in review. This takes a little bit of setting up. You'll want to have the students use their cameras or mobile devices to take pictures and videos throughout the year. During the final month before the term ends, upload the collection of footage to a WeVideo project, and let the editing fun begin. As a group, decide on a class theme, select the video transitions, and add text inserts. Debut the video at the end of the course. The video can serve as a review of the content that was covered or to highlight the students' favorite learning moments. Just for fun, students can also create a second video with bloopers or outtakes that celebrate the lighter side of classroom interactions.

weVIDEO

Tweet Tweet: What Fellow Educators Are Saying

WeVideo is an easy-to-use, feature-rich, online video editing tool that lets students work collaboratively on video projects from any computer. Integrates very well with Google Drive and has excellent tutorials to get students using it quickly.

Kyle Pace (@kylepace)

WeVideo is a fantastic Cloud-based video production solution for educators and students. It allows multiple users to edit the same product and incorporate graphics, music, and effects. Sharing is a snap, and free accounts are available.

Sandi Dennis (@sandidennis)

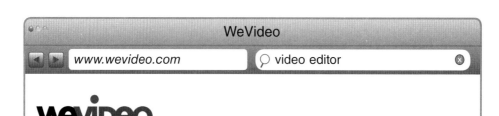

www.wevideo.com | video editor

wevideo

Quick Tip: Create your own Cousteau-style video by having students provide their own narrations to curricular videos.

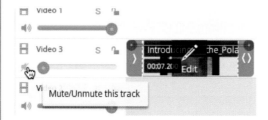

Add a video to the timeline and click the speaker icon to mute the audio.

Click "Record" to use webcam to capture your student's narration.

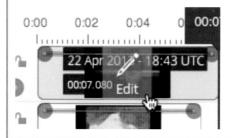

Add their clip to the timeline and click "Edit."

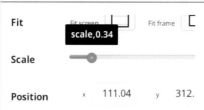

Adjust the scale to create a "picture-in-picture" effect.

Position   x   111.04   y   312.

(You can also drag the media to the right using the Hand icon)

🎞 See WeVideo in Action

Visit the online community at www.untanglingthewebcommunity.com.

3

PRESENTATION TOOLS
Life Beyond PowerPoint

How many bullet points does it take to kill an audience?

We've all been there. Sitting through a never-ending in-service or workshop as the presenter reads through every word of a PowerPoint slide. And as the session drags on, it becomes painfully obvious that sharing information effectively is nearly as important as having significant information to share. Traditionally, these presentations are comprised of a presenter sharing a series of visuals to support their message. For more than twenty years, the de facto method of providing those visuals has been PowerPoint. Keynote provides a viable alternative for Mac users, but outside of cosmetic differences, the end product is virtually identical. In recent years, there have been a series of web tools released that are beginning to challenge the status quo and expand the presentation genre dramatically.

There are obvious benefits to using web-based presentation tools, such as cost, convenience, and platform flexibility. More significantly, online presentation tools have shifted the way we use the visual medium to communicate. Rather than creating material that is intended to be supplemental to a live presenter, the visuals are now being created in a way that are intended to stand on their own—with or without an audio accompaniment.

PowerPoint is a medium that has always been intended to be used as a series of linear visuals supporting what a presenter is sharing verbally. As self-publishing gained in popularity, the need for effective ways to save those presentations and share them online arose. Some sites created simple platforms for uploading existing presentations, converting them and sharing them out in a variety of ways. Others changed the model itself, providing tools to create presentations that can stand alone, combining images and audio in a self-running format online. While most stayed true to the linear format that dominated the presentation genre, a few tools attempted to break new ground and veer away from that tradition entirely.

These sites have opened up new avenues of sharing out information for teachers and students. It is easy to look at them and see nothing more than support for live presenters. However, they can also be a publishing platform for student projects—with or without the live component. A presentation created solely to exist on its own, without a person talking over it, will have very different requirements to be effective. Things that might be spoken aloud need to be put into writing, and the balance between content and design is even more challenging to maintain. The key is to stop thinking about them as a presentation engine and to visualize them as a publishing platform.

Just as with traditional assignments, students need to focus on what content they want to share first. Once that has been identified, the audience must be considered, as well as the method of delivery. A project that will solely be shared online will have different requirements than one that will be presented in person as well as shared afterward. If the primary audience is in the room but resources will need to be shared later, SlideShare provides one of the simplest, most effective ways to manage that. If a student will be presenting for their peers, but want their presentation to be effective even without their voice-over, Prezi may be an ideal choice. VoiceThread excels at providing a contained, self-running online presentation but isn't well suited to supporting a live presenter. As with most web tools, they may lack in breadth but make up for this by excelling in the singular experience that they do offer.

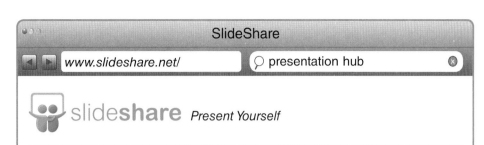

SlideShare

www.slideshare.net/   ⊘ presentation hub   ✕

slideshare *Present Yourself*

Teachers are natural presenters, sharing information in front of an audience (their class) on a daily basis. Prior to modern presentation software, the overhead projector was the dominant technology, allowing teachers to project handwritten or typed acetate slides. Once presentation software became popular in the 1990s and digital projectors overtook the overhead projector as a common classroom tool, digital presentations became a mainstay for sharing curricular information. In contrast to the many ways that slides can be created for the classroom, SlideShare is a social hub that allows you to upload and share your presentations with educators around the globe.

SlideShare has an incredible library of shared presentations. In addition to PowerPoint and Keynote presentations, users can share PDFs, Word documents, and much more. The site has been around for several years now and has stayed current by offering deep integration with social networks such as Facebook and LinkedIn. This does more than make it simple to share content with people you are connected to; it also helps you discover content that your colleagues have liked, viewed, and posted. Like many of the tools written about in this book, SlideShare allows users to comment on and "Favorite" the content that you find.

SlideShare just converts your presentation for online viewing. It's up to you to create compelling content.

Perhaps the most exciting feature of SlideShare is the online functionality it adds to presentations. Once

www.slideshare.net/ | ○ presentation hub

 slide**share**

content is posted, it is converted by the site and displayed through their online viewer. Instead of just providing a link to download the file, visitors can flip directly through the content itself. Additionally, you are provided with an embed code to place the presentation within another site, such as a class homepage or a blog. This portability of the content makes sharing the presentation simple.

There is a huge repository of educational presentations on the site ranging from conference sessions to classroom lessons and student projects that educators have chosen to share with the community.

The content on the site is community-policed, meaning that if content is objectionable or spam it is up to the users to flag it as such. While there is a potential for finding inappropriate content on the site, actual occurrences of this are minimal. Of course, teachers should test the waters themselves to determine if the content on the site is appropriate for their specific group of students.

189 Followers

 teach42
3 presentations
Following 2, 12 followers

 Julie Lindsay
Director at Flat Classroom
43 presentations, 2 documents
Following 123, 185 followers

 arvino_mudjiarto
Following 37, 22 followers

If you find a presentation you like, follow the person who created it. You'll be notified whenever they upload something new.

SlideShare has done a great job of keeping up with the times by adding new sharing options and a wider view of what they consider a presentation. Videos are now being accepted by the site, giving you the flexibility to share a video of a presentation or to share a narrated version of the presentation. You can even embed YouTube videos directly inside a SlideShare presentation so viewers won't be forced to navigate away from your content just to view the video.

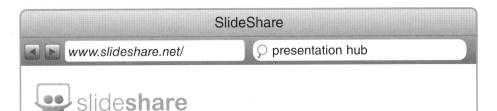

Embedding is a simple process. Choose the size, copy the code, and paste it into your own webpage.

Crafting a great presentation takes a lot of time and effort. SlideShare allows you to contribute your presentations to a community of educators that are eager to learn from your efforts. SlideShare works well on mobile devices, which gives you the flexibility to watch and share presentations on the go.

Classroom Idea— On-Demand Professional Development

SlideShare makes it possible to be in two places at once . . . kind of. If you are at a conference and forced to decide between two sessions you want to attend, SlideShare just might provide a solution for you. Many presenters are using SlideShare as a way to share digital handouts or even the actual slides they will be presenting. Search for the name of the conference or presenters, and you might be pleasantly surprised by just how many sessions are sharing their resources via SlideShare. Whether you're at the conference in person or following it from afar, be sure to check out SlideShare for some of the great presentations that you may be missing out on.

Kick It Up a Notch—Combo Time!

SlideShare is a great tool by itself. But it can be even more powerful when combined with other online apps. Let's take a look at a project that your students can do when they mash up SlideShare, Big Huge Labs, and Kidblog.

The next time your students need to create a presentation, have them start off in Big Huge Labs. Use the tools there to create visual aids that can replace bullet-heavy slides. Once the presentation is created, we're going to pass it

| ◄ ► | www.slideshare.net/ | 🔍 presentation hub |

slideshare

through SlideShare enroute to Kidblog. Upload the presentation into SlideShare, grab the embed code, and have the students add it to a blog post. They should add notes about how they created the presentation and any information the reader should know about it prior to viewing. The presentation can now be shared with other classes next door, down the block, or around the globe—with viewers sharing their feedback through comments.

slideshare

Tweet Tweet: What Fellow Educators Are Saying

For anyone regularly using slidedecks, this provides the perfect archive as well as great inspiration from others.

Dean Shareski (@shareski)

SlideShare allowed my students to take their Spanish presentations out of the class and share with a larger community. They became producers of knowledge to a wider audience.

Michelle Wendt (@meechele7)

SlideShare facilitates content personalization and generates discussion. The versatile nature of SlideShare's publishing platform and its ease of use is perfect for showcasing learning, making it a staple in my project based learning toolkit.

Jennifer Dorman (@cliotech)

SlideShare

www.slideshare.net/   🔍 presentation hub   ⊗

slideshare

Quick Tip: Add a voice-over to your presentation by uploading an audio track.

🔊 Add audio

After uploading a presentation, click on "Add audio."

Upload an mp3 audio file from your computer

Note: we do not host music files, only recordings of a presenter talking an
Please wait for a few moments if you don't see the orange "Upload" butt

Upload mp3 file...

Select a narration track from your computer (must be prerecorded).

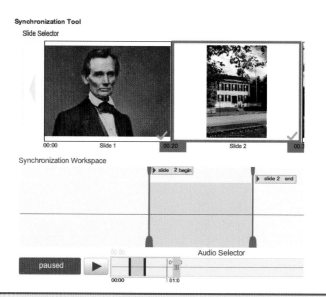

Select each slide, and choose entry and exit points on the timeline.

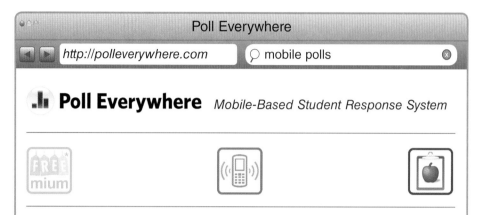

Poll Everywhere

.Ili Poll Everywhere *Mobile-Based Student Response System*

Many of the tools we've chosen to include in this book were picked because they are elegant in their simplicity. While Poll Everywhere can be simple, the deeper you dig, the more features you'll discover. At its heart, it's a response system that's intended to be used with mobile devices. You ask a question (open ended or multiple choice), and students can respond through text messaging.

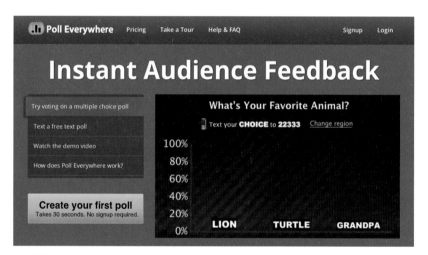

Poll Everywhere's home page lets you get started with instant polls . . . well, in an instant.

If you want to try out the site, you can create a free poll right from their home page. Enter in your question(s), add the answers (if it is to be multiple choice), and click submit. You'll be brought to a page that displays directions for how people can vote. As each answer arrives, the responses show up immediately on the screen. This can create dramatic tension as the bar graph displaying the answers swings back and forth with the incoming votes!

.ɪₗ Poll Everywhere

For many educators, that's all they need the site to do, and they never try any other features. However, that's barely scratching the surface of what's available through Poll Everywhere. If you look closely at the voting page, you'll see that the site also allows people to vote via the web for those that don't have unlimited texting plans. From that same page, you also have a robust ability to customize the on-screen display, to download the poll into PowerPoint or Keynote, to allow voting via Twitter, to share the poll via popular social sites and blogs, and to do much more. Once you have signed in, you can create series of polls to be used for a class, moderate responses as they come in, and view the results via the web.

That's all through the free teacher account, which allows for up to forty votes per poll. If you choose to upgrade to a paid plan, you gain access to many new features for deeper functionality and customization. You are able to import student names and generate reports based on student responses. You can even establish what the correct answers are for multiple choice or true/false questions and have the site automatically grade student responses. Subscribers also unlock the ability to use custom keywords in their polls, which makes responding much more user friendly. There are two tiers for paid education subscriptions—one for individual teachers and another option for schools.

▼ How People Can Respond

☑ Text messages from the US – Education

☐ Web devices on PollEv.com/teach42 (?)

☐ Tweets to @teach42 (?)

☑ Private link (?)
Try it now

> Answer polls using phones, laptops, tablets, or any other internet-connected device.

While Poll Everywhere can be used spur of the moment, it works best when planned ahead of time. Teachers can create polls for their lessons and use them to check for understanding, allow student input, and provide every student the chance to respond to every question. Inserting polls throughout a class period helps keep students engaged by breaking up lessons into chunks and providing them with actions that don't disrupt the flow of the class. Best of all, the responses are immediate so if a lesson isn't reaching them, teachers can make adjustments immediately.

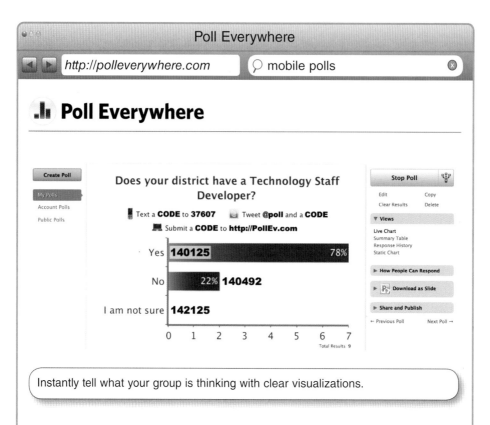

Instantly tell what your group is thinking with clear visualizations.

Poll Everywhere has become extremely popular with teachers whose schools have embraced a **BYOD** (bring your own device) initiative. It enables them to integrate a wide variety of mobile devices into a lesson without creating a classroom management nightmare. The teacher doesn't need to be familiar with the student devices to build the polls for each lesson. It's a simple way to dive into the initiative and get some easy successes under your belt.

Classroom Idea—Polling Beyond the Classroom

While Poll Everywhere is ideally suited to classroom use, it can also be a valuable way to gather feedback from teachers as well as parents. Using polls during faculty meetings allows the audience to be active participants rather than passive recipients. An obvious use with parents would be at an open house, but it can even be used to make newsletters more interactive. Add an open-ended question to your newsletter along with instructions for how to respond. For example, if your students are studying syllables, you might include, "Throughout the weekend, send a text message documenting every four-syllable word you see." Review the results with the class on Monday as an informal assessment.

Poll Everywhere

Kick It Up a Notch—Poll Results Makeover

Most people view the results of open-ended polls using the "Live Text Wall" because it enables you to see the results appear in real time. Very few ever take the time to poke around the display settings. If you do, you'll find the ability to change the theme. Instead of having answers drop down from the top, you can have them scroll across like a "Live Ticker" or float around the screen in bubbles through the "Colorize" theme. One of the most effective ways to display the results of an open-ended poll is to make use of the "Word Cloud" option under "Views." When you select that feature, it will display a text box that contains all of the responses that have been sent in at that point. Click inside the box, copy the text (Ctrl+C or Cmd+C), and use the links below it to paste the results directly into Wordle. A couple of clicks later and the results of your poll are displayed in a simple, attractive manner with the most frequently used words appearing the largest.

http://polleverywhere.com   🔍 mobile polls   ⊗

.ıl Poll Everywhere

Tweet Tweet: **What Fellow Educators Are Saying**

> A great and inexpensive tool for formative assessment. It has all the benefits of clickers with none of the expense.

Tom Whitby (@tomwhitby)

> With embeddable slides, you can quickly assess during presentations and combat misconceptions. Great tool for increasing participation.

Bob Abrams (@misterabrams)

> I love using Poll Everywhere during class to get students engaged in the material. They are really attentive and interested because we are meeting them on a technology level that they use every day!

Doug Butchy (@dougbutchy)

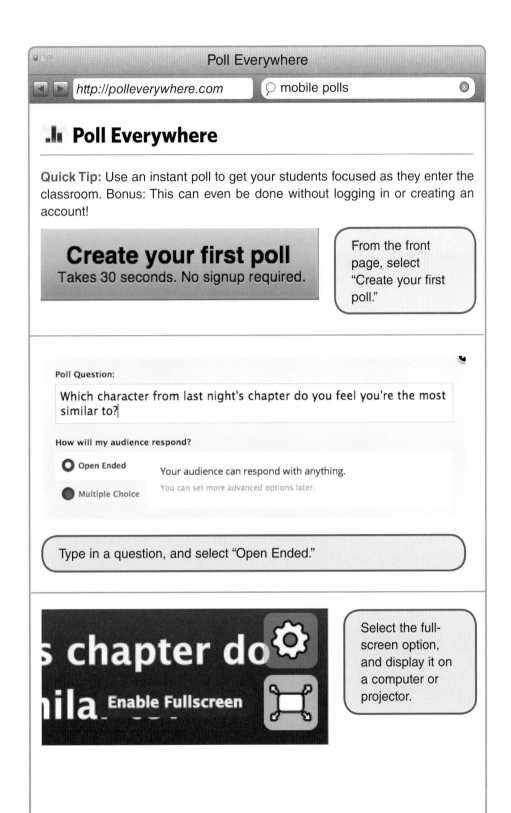

http://polleverywhere.com   🔍 mobile polls

.Ⅱ Poll Everywhere

Quick Tip: Use an instant poll to get your students focused as they enter the classroom. Bonus: This can even be done without logging in or creating an account!

Create your first poll
Takes 30 seconds. No signup required.

From the front page, select "Create your first poll."

Poll Question:

Which character from last night's chapter do you feel you're the most similar to?

How will my audience respond?

⦿ **Open Ended** — Your audience can respond with anything.
You can set more advanced options later.

⦿ **Multiple Choice**

Type in a question, and select "Open Ended."

s chapter do ⚙

ila **Enable Fullscreen** ⛶

Select the full-screen option, and display it on a computer or projector.

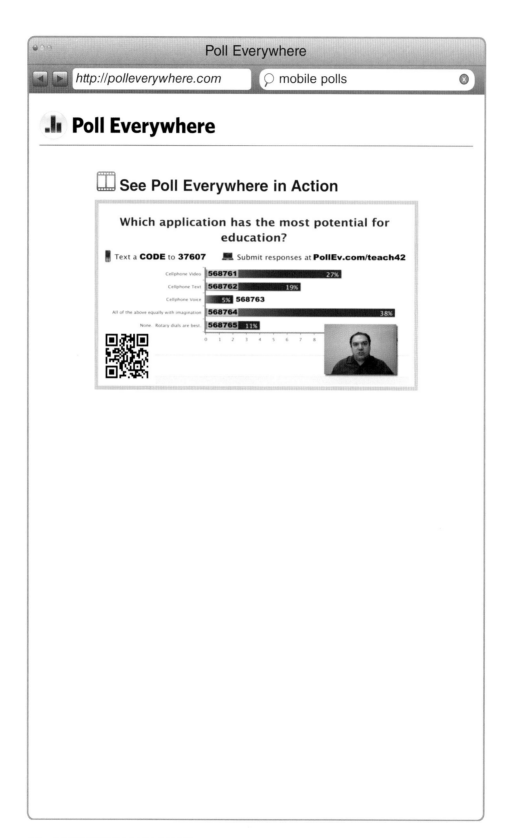

http://voicethread.com   🔍 collaborative slideshows ⊗

voicethread *Collaborative Voices in the Cloud*

The rate at which new online apps have evolved has created an environment where people are constantly searching for the next great thing. It is increasingly difficult for sites to maintain their relevancy for the long term when new competitors are released every few months. This is why VoiceThread's success over time is all the more significant. The site was released in 2005, which makes it a patriarch in the EdTech community. While some sites are in rapid development, with new features showing up every time you log in, VoiceThread has stayed remarkably true to its original vision. While they continue to make improvements, such as an iOS app and Facebook photo imports, on the whole the interface has changed little since the early years. Among the sea of sites that are constantly in flux, the reliability of VoiceThread is why it is so trusted by educators.

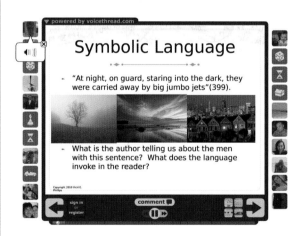

This VoiceThread was created from an uploaded slideshow and the people's faces surrounding the slide represent audio, text, and video comments on the content.

VoiceThread is based on a fairly simple concept: sharing photos and videos online along with the ability to comment on them. The interface may seem dated, but it has proved to be highly intuitive to both teachers and students. Like many other Web 2.0 sites, the simplicity of the interface does not indicate a lack of depth. On the contrary, the commenting system allows educators to make use of the site for a wide variety of projects at all grade levels.

http://voicethread.com  ○ collaborative slideshows

voicethread

There are three steps to creating a project. The first is to import your media. Your options include adding via URL, uploading from your computer, and adding a video or digital photo directly from your webcam. You also have the option of importing from your Flickr or Facebook account or selecting from nearly 700,000 images in the New York Public Library's Digital Gallery. Most VoiceThreads consist of images with a few making use of the option to add videos to a project. However, there are several other file types that can be imported into projects and rarely seem to be mentioned by VoiceThread's evangelists. Audio files (podcasts, speeches, songs), Word documents, spreadsheets, PDFs, and even PowerPoints can all be added to a VoiceThread. Presentations will even be split up into the individual slides upon import. These options provide much richer options for using VoiceThread in higher grade levels than many may realize.

Once the media has been added to the project, the next step is to add commentary to it. The options available here are what separates VoiceThread from other slideshow apps in the space. Comments can be text, voice, or video. Text comments are the most basic, added simply via typing. Audio comments can be recorded directly into the site, uploaded (for premium subscribers) or recorded via telephone (minutes are limited). Video comments are recorded through the user's webcam. With all flavors of commenting, users also have the option of adding annotations to the media in the slide. After selecting a color, users can draw freely on the screen, highlighting key elements or adding notes to the slide. What makes this feature remarkable is that when paired with an audio or video comment, the annotations are displayed in real time. As a teacher or student provides the voice-over to a slide, their marks on the screen will be displayed in time with their comments. In a sense, the functionality is similar to the screencasting stylings of Khan Academy videos. Every frame can be commented on and the order can be rearranged as needed.

The final step of the process is sharing. Projects can be embedded into blogs, shared via link, or even exported as videos. Sharing via link is where you can control both the degree of privacy and the options for collaboration. Users can choose whether anyone (anybody who has or sees the link to this project) can view the VoiceThread as well as whether it will be listed in the general gallery, accessible to the entire VoiceThread community. Users can also select whether visitors will be able to add their own comments to the project and whether those comments will be posted immediately or after being approved by the owner.

voicethread

While there are only four checkboxes in the "Get a Link" box, these options are what enable educators to determine how open or private the project will be and the degree of interactivity that will be allowed. With a paid educator account, teachers can share projects privately among their groups, classes, or school.

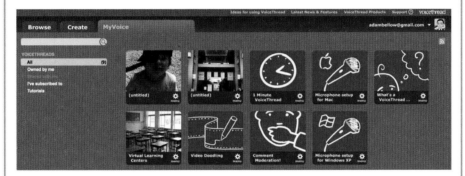

When you're signed into VoiceThread, you can access your own content as well as content that has been shared with you.

It may seem easy to dismiss VoiceThread as an overglorified slideshow, but the commenting structure takes it far beyond that. The ability to add both audio and video comments makes it an incredibly viable platform for digital storytelling. The interface works equally well for kindergarten students narrating their journal entries as it does for secondary students summarizing the finer points of classic literature. Allowing visitors to add comments transforms it from a traditional publishing engine into a collaborative environment for sharing. It is frequently used for projects where students are connecting with peers on a global level. By creating a simple framework with open-ended questions, students can encourage visitors to view responses from others and participate by adding their own audio-, video-, or text-based comments.

Like many of our favorite Web 2.0 tools, the site is incredibly simple from a technical perspective and yet robust enough that educators of all subjects and grade levels can leverage it to achieve powerful results. Unlike most other sites, VoiceThread has proved that it is not only stable but that it is able to maintain its relevancy over time. Basic accounts are free, but users are limited to saving five projects. Upon request, educators can receive an upgrade to the free K–12 VoiceThread Educator account that allows them to save up to fifty

voicethread

projects. Upgrading to a paid Single Educator, School, or District license provides significant benefits, including the ability to create student accounts, save unlimited projects, and use credits to archive VoiceThreads offline as videos. The diversity of proven track record, options, and education-friendly features have made VoiceThread a perennial favorite amongst educators.

Recording a comment is easy. You can type it, record audio or video from a webcam, and even call a phone number to record audio.

Classroom Idea—Annotated Journaling

Until students are proficient at writing, journaling involves drawing pictures and adding as much commentary as they are able. Often the student will describe their work while the teacher transcribes it on the page. In place of this, have students create an individual VoiceThread journal and use the webcam to take a photo of their work. After holding up their picture and letting VoiceThread snap a copy of it, students will record themselves describing the page via video or audio. Every week, parents can visit the site to see what new pages their student has added.

Kick It Up a Notch—Continuing the Conversation at Home

One of the challenges when learning a new language is mastering the use of it in a conversational setting. VoiceThread provides an ideal platform for combining listening, watching, and responding to prompts from the teacher. In a series of slides, the instructor can share a variety of questions and challenges for the students. As homework, their job is to view each question, formulate a response, and then post it as a video comment. While the first student will only see their own response posted, future students will be able to review their classmates' answers before adding their own. An added bonus of this sort of assignment is that the teacher is able to review the class's homework prior to the start of class the next day.

◀ ▶ | *http://voicethread.com* | ○ collaborative slideshows | ⊗

voicethread

Tweet Tweet: What Fellow Educators Are Saying

VoiceThread allows me to introduce my students to a topic before class. I often crack a joke or give a tip for bonus points to make sure they watch the thread before class. Starting class already knowing the basics has allowed my students to soar.

Dr. Cynthia Vavasseur (@drvav)

VoiceThread is used in all of our Spanish classes in the high school to allow students to practice what they have learned in class, comment on each others work and allow for collaborative learning. VoiceThread is inexpensive, easy to maintain and set up users/groups and is integrated into our Haiku Learning Management System.

Lisa Abel-Palmieri (@Learn21Tech)

VoiceThread is the most flexible, useful tool I've found for students to use. I use it with first graders but friends use it with college students. It fosters sharing, communication, and collaboration.

Jennifer Orr (@jenorr)

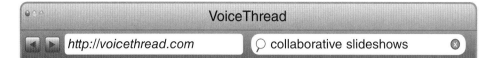

http://voicethread.com   🔍 collaborative slideshows   ⊗

voicethread

Quick Tip: There's more to VoiceThread comments than just talking. Liven up your comments by adding annotations or even navigating through slides.

Click on "comment" to open up the options for adding text and voice to a slide.

Click record to begin leaving an audio comment.

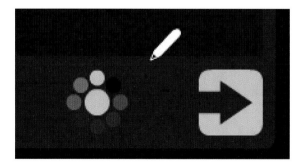

As you record, you can draw annotations or even use the arrows to navigate to other slides. Everything you do will stay in sync with your voice when people listen to it later.

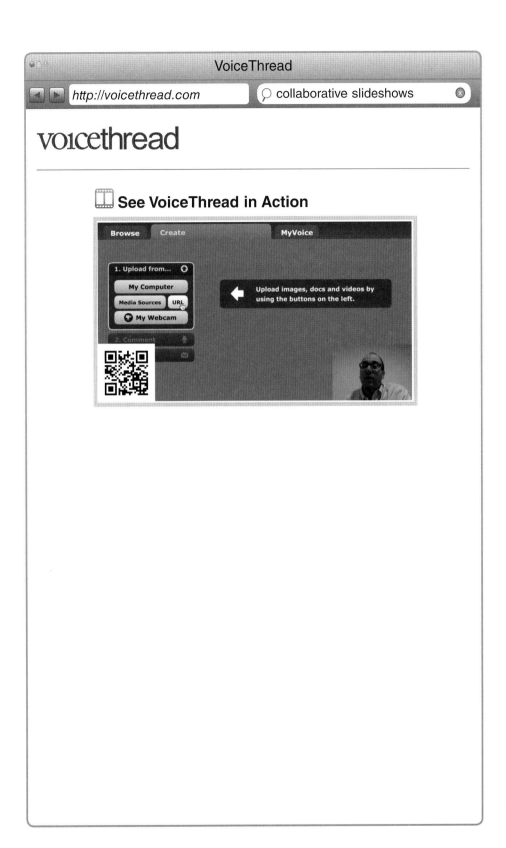

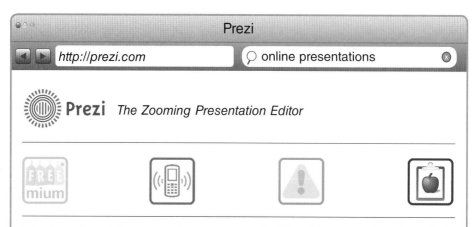

Prezi *The Zooming Presentation Editor*

You never forget the moment you see your first Prezi. You are sitting in a chair, bracing yourself for yet another traditional slide-based presentation. The opening slide is on the screen. But when the presenter clicks through to the next slide . . . there is no actual slide. Instead, the screen just zooms over to the next piece of content. It's not so much of a transition as a shift. And regardless of the value of the content being presented, the question that resides in the back of your head is "How are they DOING that?"

Prezi is not your grandpa's PowerPoint.

Prezi was one of the first sites to really demonstrate that presentations could be so much more than just the typical PowerPoint. Traditionally, presentations are comprised of a series of slides. While there may be a variety of transitions and animations available, the basic format is always slide-based. When Prezi was released, it broke from the mold so dramatically that it immediately became the de facto alternative to traditional presentations. While the information being shared can still be sequential or linear, the layout itself is

Prezi

an open canvas. Instead of chunking content into separate segments, creators can think more holistically about their topic. It allows them to step back and consider, "What is the overarching theme of my presentation, and how can I represent that visually?" Presentations about economics began being laid out on Monopoly boards, projects related to global issues might zoom around a map of the world, and science content could be embedded directly into ecosystems and biomes. Users embedded their content within the larger canvas and then laid out a path that didn't just move side to side or up and down but also zoomed in and out as needed.

It cannot be overstated just how much Prezi differs from the software that preceded it. While the others all focused in on new transitions, shadow effects, and increasingly obscure features, Prezi opts for simplicity. I remember seeing a tweet from a kindergarten teacher that read "Just taught my students how to create PowerPoint presentations." Can you even imagine a five-year-old looking at PowerPoint and trying to make sense of it? Consider how confusing and intimidating the interface would be. To do something as simple as change the size of some text, the students need to select the text, click and drag to highlight it, find the size selector (which is often on a separate menu tab), and then select a number. What do those numbers represent? How big is "18" to a young student?

Prezi offers a dramatically different solution to this. When selecting an object, users can drag the corners to make the object larger or smaller. There is no number associated with it. You just make the object the size you want. It's radically different but so simple it seems astonishing that nobody thought of it before. Prezi may be missing dozens or even hundreds of options that full-featured software solutions offer, but more than likely you won't miss many of them.

One of other dramatic ways that Prezi breaks from the norm is that presentations do not have to be linear. While it may be possible to create a nonlinear presentation in PowerPoint, it requires an enormous amount of planning and effort. After laying out the content on a canvas, a Prezi user can draw out a path to click through it. At any time, the user can click and drag on the canvas itself to navigate through the information laid out in the presentation. Click on any object, and you instantly zoom in on that specific content. There are keyboard

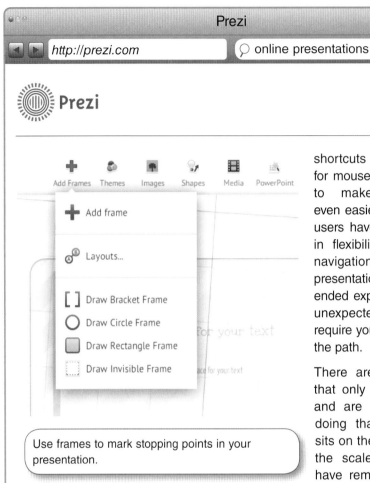

Use frames to mark stopping points in your presentation.

shortcuts and support for mouse scroll wheels to make navigation even easier. In this way, users have the ultimate in flexibility: structured navigation for formal presentations and open-ended exploration when unexpected questions require you to stray from the path.

There are many sites that only do one thing and are satisfied with doing that well. Prezi sits on the other end of the scale. While they have remained true to their original vision—transforming presentations—they have consistently added new innovations that keep breaking ground in the presentation space. To make longtime PowerPoint users more comfortable, they added the ability to import previously created presentations as well as a path viewer that looks remarkably similar to the traditional PowerPoint slide-based navigator. They were the first presentation tool to add in the ability to navigate through 3-D backgrounds, such that when you zoom in on a background canvas, it can actually transition to the next level deeper in space (think of a canvas that lets you zoom into the sky and not only break through the clouds but to continue on into space). When a user adds a YouTube hyperlink, it immediately embeds the video itself into the presentation. There is a PDF exporter for printing, the ability to edit and play Prezis offline, an iPad viewer, and a plethora of themes to start from. Users can allow others to copy their presentations, essentially making their Prezi a customizable template for others.

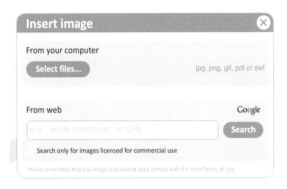

You can add your own content (images, videos, links, etc.) or even search for images right from the site.

One of the most interesting additions, though, is Prezi Meeting. This feature provides two key capabilities for educators. It allows users to share out a link and present their Prezi to viewers online. As the presenter navigates through the presentation, everybody who has it loaded in their own browser will follow the same path in real time. The flip side of this feature, though, is the ability for up to ten users to edit a Prezi collaboratively at the same time. It's almost like inviting ten artists to all paint on the same canvas. Each user is represented by a small avatar, which allows other editors to know what they are working on. A group of people can add, edit, and manipulate a presentation in real time without stepping on each other's toes.

Prezi provides premium accounts to educators for free, as well as an educator Pro account with extras like offline editing and increased storage space for a small monthly fee. Both educator accounts provide users the ability to remove Prezi branding from presentations and to save their projects privately. Prezi also has a robust education community called Prezi U, which features educators around the globe sharing ideas and projects for others to be inspired by.

Classroom Idea—Make Venn Diagrams Come Alive

Prezi can be a very effective way to display a variety of information, but the way you can lay information out on a canvas and then zoom into it makes it ideal for deeper dives into data sets. Students can use the frame tool to create a Venn diagram, using as many circles as needed. Have the students

each take turns (using the meeting feature or taking turns at a computer) importing images to populate each section of the diagram. Have students come up to the front and click on their contributions, explaining their choice and why it fits that specific set.

Kick It Up a Notch—Choose Your Own Adventure

Many people create a linear path for their Prezi's, marking specific points for the viewer to navigate through. However, you shouldn't be afraid to stray from the path! Go back in time and have your students exercise both their literary skills and their flowcharting abilities by creating a choose-your-own-adventure-inspired story. Start by creating a flowchart of the story arc. Flesh out each step along the path with both text and supporting images. Add them in to Prezi, and use arrows to mark the path readers should navigate to get from one point to the next. It's up to the student whether the paths move from top to bottom or whether they wind up zigzagging across each other. Be sure to provide opening instructions so viewers know that they'll need to use their mouse to click and drag their way through the interactive story.

Bonus points: Just text and images? Don't forget that Prezi works great with video as well! Students could record short snippets for each event in the story and add them to the project.

Double bonus points: Use the meeting feature to have groups of students create a collaborative story together!

http://prezi.com   ○ online presentations   ⊗

 Prezi

Tweet Tweet: What Fellow Educators Are Saying

When Prezi added the collaboration feature, WOW did presentations in my class change! It gives ability to be more free, creative, and collaborative than with traditional PowerPoint.

Amber Bridge (@abridgesmith)

Light years beyond PowerPoint, Prezi enables units to be taught from one place! Link YouTube, Google Images, and Graphic Organizers with a click of the mouse—great for teachers and students of all tech abilities.

Kristina Wambold (@MrsWambold)

Students love the creativity this allows them. Helps them understand presentation of key ideas and how concepts can flow.

Robin McLean (@rcmclean)

Prezi

http://prezi.com | 🔍 online presentations ⊗

Prezi

Quick Tip: Have an image, video, or block of text that you want to use across several Prezis? Add it to your Object Library.

Select the item that you want to save and right click on it (Cmd+click on OS X). Choose "Add to Object Library."

When you want to use that object in a new Prezi, select "Open Object Library" from the navigation bar along the top.

Select the object (image, video, text, etc.) that you want to use and click "Insert." A copy of it will be added to your project.

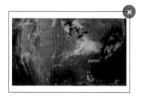

http://prezi.com | online presentations ⓧ

Prezi

🎞 See Prezi in Action

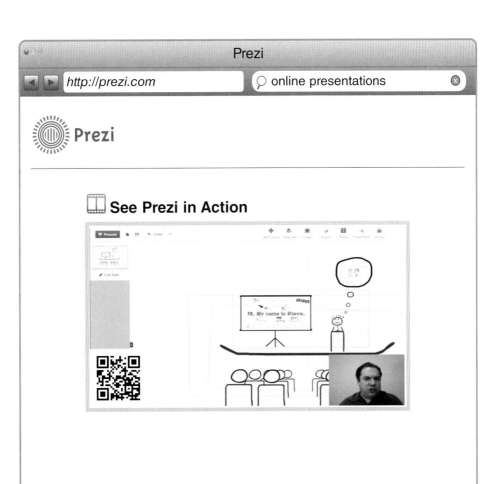

4

SOCIAL NETWORKING TOOLS

Talk, Text, and Learn Together

Depending on your age (or level of geekiness) you may not recall the beginning of the social web. Living through a period of constant change sometimes makes it difficult to take note of what is happening while the shift is occurring—but looking back it is shocking to see just how far we have come in such a short period of time.

One can argue that the web itself, a series of digital connections made between machines, is social. Perhaps that is true, but it is just the technological foundation that paved the way for what we think of as the modern web. Just think of the many different new forms of communication that have stemmed from the ability for machines to connect and send packets of data back and forth. The ways that we as a society are able to connect are astounding. The world has changed a great deal in the past two decades, and there are certainly no indications this rapid evolution will be slowing anytime soon.

Growing up, we watched shows like *The Jetsons* that were showcasing seemingly impossible technologies, such as videoconferences between people. We now live in a reality that enables videoconferencing to anywhere in the world from devices that have no wires and fit in our pockets and purses. It is incredible to think of all these ways we are able to connect and even more powerful to look at all the ways we can bring this technology into the classroom for both ourselves and our students to use.

Social networks and schools sometimes cause folks to feel a little uneasy because of mainstream news reports of what can go wrong when people connect online. However, we feel that social media is an invaluable tool that our students will be relying on for the foreseeable future and for good reason. Being part of a global network and knowing the value that one can derive from it is a cornerstone of being "a 21st century good digital citizen." Being social online—and having that behavior modeled appropriately in schools—is an important part of providing the best education for a student today.

Some may argue that social networking is the antithesis of the type of social-emotional development that should be occurring in schools. The social web is not intended to replace face-to-face interactions but to supplement it and provide more opportunities to extend those relationships. Working in a room full of different students is an excellent way to learn collaboration and social skills. In a similar way, interacting in virtual rooms enhances their ability to collaborate online—beyond physical barriers. From this perspective, it seems strange that many schools ban or limit the social connections that their students have online.

No matter what side of the argument you fall into, there are wonderful web tools available today that let students create a presence for themselves online and to craft their own digital identities. These social tools give all students a chance to have their opinions heard and to explore ideas with other students and educators.

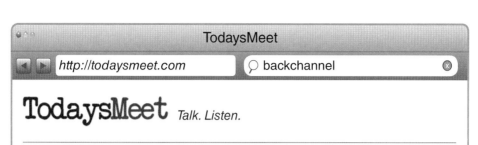

TodaysMeet *Talk. Listen.*

TodaysMeet allows a teacher to create a private **back channel** that can be used as a collaborative means for discussing and documenting classroom interactions. TodaysMeet is one of the simplest tools you will read about in this book. You can be up and running in about the same amount of time it took you to read this sentence. That said, it is a powerful communication tool and can help change the dynamic of a classroom.

TodaysMeet

Talk. Listen.

TodaysMeet helps you embrace the backchannel and connect with your audience in realtime.

Encourage the room to use the live stream to make comments, ask questions, and use that feedback to tailor your presentation, sharpen your points, and address audience needs.

Create a Room.

Name your room

EdTech
ie: **http://todaysmeet.com/EdTec** ✓

Delete the room in

one week
how long will the room data be saved?

By submitting this form you agree to the Privacy Policy and Terms.

Create your Room.

Blog | About | Help | Privacy | Terms of Use | © 2008–2012 James Socol.

To get started with TodaysMeet, simply name your room, and select how long you wish to keep the chat open.

You might be asking yourself, "What would I use a back channel for?" Back channels are communication boards (private or public) that students and teachers can use to converse in real time. It can be an excellent way to focus conversation around a specific topic or to use as a virtual meeting space where students can ask questions and provide assistance to each other.

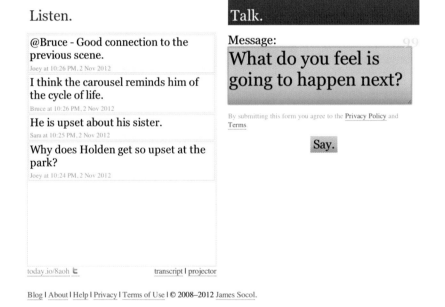

While many schools are embracing social media on an institutional level, others limit their students' participation with tools that allow real-time web-based communication. TodaysMeet addresses many common concerns by allowing this type of communication in a controlled environment. Teachers can provide clear expectations of good netiquette and model meaningful social interactions online. Rather than blocking students from communicating on the web, teachers can provide students with clear guidelines and help them discover how social tools can enhance the learning process.

Having a TodaysMeet back channel running in your class is a great way to allow all student voices to be heard.

Using TodaysMeet with your students provides each learner with the opportunity to be part of the conversation. Students who are not comfortable raising their hands may be willing to share through comments in a classroom

chat. This method of communication can create a level playing field and allow all voices to be heard. While it provides students with a platform for questions and answers, it also allows you as the teacher to play the role of moderator, providing guidance and prodding students as needed.

We said it was easy, but how easy is it? Head to TodaysMeet.com, enter your name and a name for your room (e.g., "Room32"). The URL will be based on the name you supply (in this case http://todaysmeet.com/Room32), which will be the link your students use to access the chat. Don't lose this URL! It is the only way to get to the room you have created and is private to the people you give it out to.

That's all there is to it! If you like, you can monitor the discussion from a mobile device or click on the "projector" button to take it into a full-screen mode. The "transcript" feature lets you view a recap of all the comments that have been shared in a print-friendly format.

Classroom Idea—Asking Questions In Class and Out

When you are introducing a new topic and want to gauge the students' understanding of what you are showing them, you can use TodaysMeet to collect their questions. Use those as discussion points, or turn those questions into the basis of study for the next class assignment. Since it is a web-based platform, you're not limited to the in-class questions from students. Let them use a TodaysMeet page to help each other with homework or research questions. Teachers often hear about cyberbullying and students being hypercritical of their peers online. Setting boundaries and having students use a back channel together can provide a model for appropriate use. Since you, as the teacher, would have access and moderation controls, it is a safe place to help facilitate responsible use of social commenting and group chat.

Kick It Up a Notch—Don't Chat During the Movie

Use TodaysMeet to create a discussion guide with questions that students need to answer while watching a video. Throughout the viewing, the teacher can moderate the conversation in the back channel. This turns a traditionally passive experience, watching a film, into an interactive activity that helps students engage in the material as they watch it. The output from the students can be viewed as an assessment of their in-class participation. Props go to Richard Byrne who shared this idea on his blog.

http://todaysmeet.com backchannel

TodaysMeet

Tweet Tweet: What Fellow Educators Are Saying

> Using TodaysMeet changed the dynamic of our administration and leadership meetings. Questions, conversations, and ideas can be formulated and captured in real time and archived for visiting later.

Steven W. Anderson (@web20classroom)

> Never before have I had such easy access to real-time feedback. Exit Tickets and Do Now activities can be discussed and assessed immediately. Easy to join and easy to share.

Joshua Winrotte (@coachrotte)

> This tool transforms meetings from "sit and gets" to "sit and get togethers"! The power of the room comes to life on the back channel.

Kristy Vincent (@bigpurplehat)

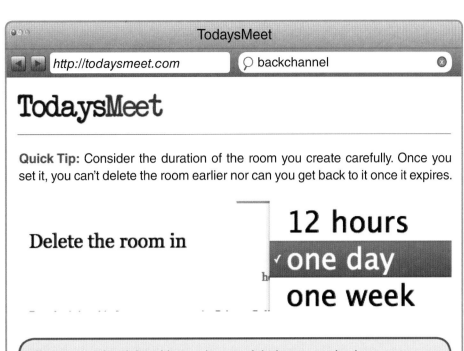

TodaysMeet

Quick Tip: Consider the duration of the room you create carefully. Once you set it, you can't delete the room earlier nor can you get back to it once it expires.

Delete the room in

12 hours
✓ one day
one week

Rooms can be deleted in two hours, eight hours, twelve hours, one day, one week, or one month. Choose wisely.

See TodaysMeet in Action

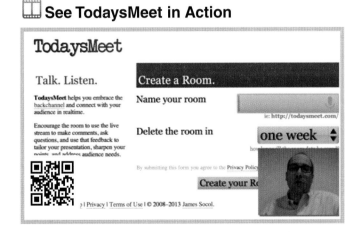

Skype in the Classroom

http://education.skype.com/   global videoconferencing

skype
in the classroom

Connect your classroom to the world. Meet new people, talk to experts, share ideas, and create amazing learning experiences.

Communication and collaboration are arguably the cornerstones of 21st-century learning—and to a larger degree, life in the 21st century. Technology has made communicating with one another easier and more affordable throughout the past two decades. Evolving from cellular calls and e-mails, we are now seeing a massive increase in the use of videoconferencing.

Skype was one of the earliest video chat and **VoIP** (voice-over Internet Protocol) technologies to gain mass adoption and is now a service that millions of people use to connect with one another daily. It truly has made the world a smaller place by allowing people of different cultures to see eye to eye. Proprietary videoconferencing units and services had been popular in education, especially the primary grades, because they enabled classrooms to connect directly to others across broad distances. These were often very good learning experiences but required all participants to have the same brand of hardware. In contrast, teachers had been making connections through blogs, local conferences, and a variety of social networks—peer to peer. There were relevant, powerful connections being made, but the method of discovery was disparate and relied on individuals to find others to connect to on their own. Skype has committed themselves to addressing that issue by creating community with the sole purpose of connecting educators and students in a simple and seamless manner.

Skype in the classroom's home page lets you search for experts or volunteer to share with others.

Skype in the classroom is designed to facilitate teachers finding other educators and experts willing to share and allows you to volunteer to do the same for other classes. The search engine tells you what level the teacher or expert is experienced with, making discovering relevant connections possible.

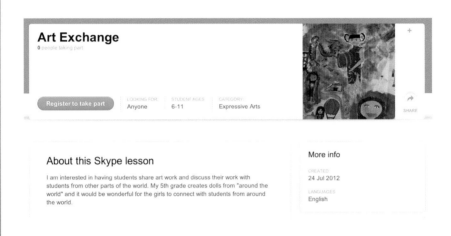

Post a project or browse for projects or lessons that help teach students about topics ranging from the arts to zoology.

Classroom Idea—Bring the Experts to YOU

Use Skype in the classroom to find an expert in an area that you are studying or to connect with the author of a book that you read in class. These real connections to professionals make a great introduction to research. Students can prepare interview questions and ask them of an expert in the field. Teachers can invite an illustrator into their classroom via Skype to talk about the work that they do and even demonstrate the creative process. You might be surprised at the wide variety of talented folks out there who are willing to share with you and your students.

Kick It Up a Notch—Students Teaching Students Teaching Students

Skype is often used to connect two classrooms from around the world. There is obvious value in connecting a class from the rural Midwest with classes in

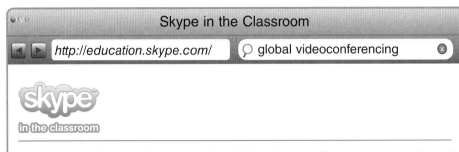

http://education.skype.com/   global videoconferencing

other areas of the world, such as the Middle East or Singapore. A meeting of the minds between vastly different cultures of students is a worthwhile experience that allows students to break down cultural barriers, exposing them to the realities of what other societies are truly like.

Mystery Skypes are a great way to learn about different people from around the globe. Let your students play twenty questions and guess where the other class/person is from.

Rather than relying on casual conversation to foster these learning experiences, flip the concept on its head and let your students step into a leadership role. Make a connection through Skype in the classroom with a teacher in another country. Have your students study that culture thoroughly through video, news articles, blogs, and other mass media. Give them ample time to explore it thoroughly enough that they don't merely understand the people of that land but that they feel they have an in-depth knowledge of their issues, concerns, and beliefs.

Through Skype, have your students present their findings to the other class. Address issues related to geography, politics, religion, and pop culture. Upon completing the presentations, allow the students in the remote classroom to respond to the presentation. Have them discuss what they got right and where they may have fallen victim to perceived stereotypes. After allowing time to discuss these issues in depth, schedule a time for the other class to follow suit, presenting their own research about the United States.

 *http://education.skype.com/* global videoconferencing

Tweet Tweet: **What Fellow Educators Are Saying**

Skype is an integral part of exploring new forms of teaching and learning. It supports a new vision of what "classrooms" can be. Saying "Hello" to someone on another continent is just the beginning, collaborating on a global team or learning from an expert or eye-witness is becoming the norm.

Silvia Tolisano (@langwitches)

Skype has allowed the students in my school to connect, collaborate, and share with other classrooms all over the country. They love to compare and contrast their personal lives with those of students in other places.

Timothy Gwynn (@tgwynn)

The greatest impact technology has in learning is connecting learners and providing new ways to learn that were not available prior to the technology. Skype allows opportunities for students to learn from and with anyone embedded in the content students are working with!

Scott Meech (@smeech)

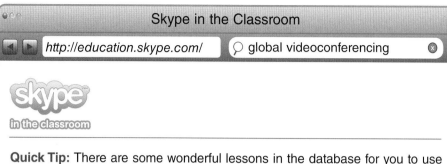

http://education.skype.com/   🔍 global videoconferencing

Quick Tip: There are some wonderful lessons in the database for you to use in your classroom. Don't forget to add your own contributions!

▦ See Skype in Action

Blogging was first introduced to the world in the late 1990s. The concept is simple; share your thoughts, creations, and opinions with the world through a series of posts published in reverse chronological order. Where most websites were organized to put the content deemed most important up front, blogs were organized to always feature the newest content. The concept of blogging has evolved and is now a mainstream medium that allows anyone in the world to be heard and interact with others.

As the Internet has matured, blogging has to accommodate a variety of formats and has evolved rapidly considering its brief history. For example, vlogs (or video blogs) are a popular way to share information these days as they require little to no writing and can be created by anyone with a video camera or webcam device. Twitter is another variation, dubbed a **microblog** due to its 140-character limit for each entry. As much as blogging has evolved, the concept remains the same; it is a platform to share with others and allow them to share back with you.

Kidblog is not the only blogging tool designed for the classroom, but it is one of the best. Kidblog allows you, as the teacher, to establish safe spaces for students to share online that can be moderated to your personal level of comfort in accordance with the mandates of your school, district, or state.

Since we are bringing up safety and moderation here, it is worth noting

Kidblog makes it simple to set up a whole blog for every one of your students.

the importance of teaching students about digital discourse and the difference between constructive feedback and hurtful teasing. Students are less likely to go astray when using a commenting system or feedback system that is being monitored by a teacher. Teachers of younger students may not feel the need to address cybercitizenship or cyberbullying directly, but at any age it is helpful to remind students that the web is an open platform and they need to be cognizant of the power their words may have over others.

What makes Kidblog such a great blogging platform for students is both the ease of use and the level of moderation it provides the teacher. With little effort, teachers can create individual student accounts and adjust the security levels based on the needs of their students. By default, the blogs that students create can only be seen by the teacher who created them. Comments and new posts can be moderated prior to showing up on the site. Comments go into a private queue until the teacher reviews them and either approves or rejects them. Teachers can choose to provide a password for parents or other guests who register on the site. Kidblog does not collect any identifying information from students, which makes it **COPPA** (Children's Online Privacy Protection Act) compliant and safe for use with students of all ages.

Kidblog not only gives students the power to write and share their ideas in the form of blog posts but also to express themselves by customizing the look and feel of their blog. They can choose from a number of different templates that not only individualize the blog but increase the students' sense of ownership. While the standard blog on Kidblog looks fine, students love to change up the appearance of their site—the same as if they were decorating their locker or doodling on the front cover of a binder.

Users familiar with WordPress blogs will be right at home in Kidblog.

Blogging is a wonderful way to share experiences, stories, journal entries, or events in your academic life and provides all learners a platform for self-expression. No matter if you use the blog as a daily, monthly, or every once in a blue moon platform, it can be a powerful way to document both living and learning.

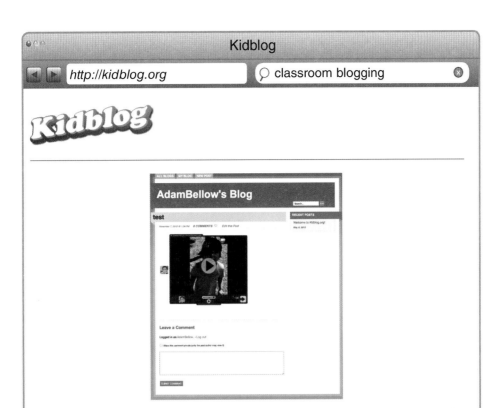

Kidblog's editor lets you embed code from other web tools in your posts.

Classroom Idea—Drop Everything and Blog

The term blog is derived from *web-log,* which originally served as a personal journal or diary of sorts. Hearkening back to its early origins, have the students establish a learning log. Use Kidblog to create an individual blog for each of your students, and set aside time each day for your students to document their learning experiences. Much like drop everything and read (DEAR) time, require students to spend time journaling on their blog at least once each week. By the end of the year, they will have roughly forty entries spanning their journey within your classroom. The blog may serve as a means for sharing personal interests, documenting classroom experiences, or even as a place for reflecting upon their own efforts, successes, and failures. These blogs often become a passion for students, a means to share

After teachers set up their class, students log in by selecting their name from the list.

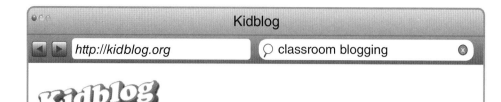

about themselves as well as to synthesize their thoughts on what they have been learning.

Kick It Up a Notch—The News In Review

Have your students visit a reputable news site and scan the headlines for an article that interests them. On their own blog, have the students write up a summary of the facts as well as their opinion about what they've shared. A simple post like this can provide them an excellent opportunity to hone their skills as a blogger. Encourage them to include a link back to the original article, to add images to the post, and to add connections to other blogs that have shared thoughts about the story.

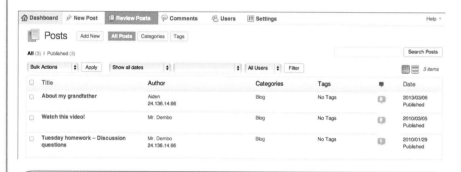

Since all students are registered under your account, you'll have one dashboard to review and/or approve their posts.

http://kidblog.org | classroom blogging

Tweet Tweet: What Fellow Educators Are Saying

Kidblog allowed me to easily give my students a personal space to share their thoughts on the class content. Freedom and ownership helped engage my students in ways I haven't seen before.

Nicholas Provenzano (@thenerdyteacher)

Kidblog is an amazing tool for elementary students. It is easy to use for both kids/teachers. My kids have an audience for their writing and can connect with the world. They are much more motivated writers. They WANT to write. #authentic

Christine Ruder (@jhox1)

Kidblog allows my students to write for a global, authentic audience and be inspired by other students, authors, and experts who take the time to comment on their blogs.

Joan Young (@flourishingkids)

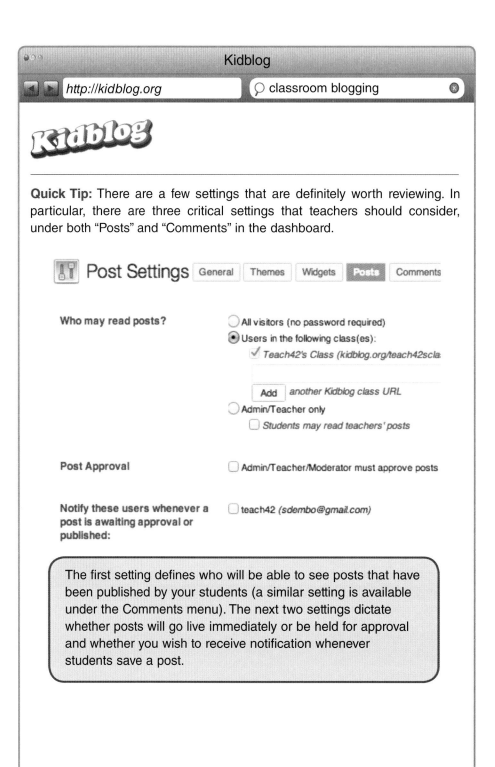

Quick Tip: There are a few settings that are definitely worth reviewing. In particular, there are three critical settings that teachers should consider, under both "Posts" and "Comments" in the dashboard.

Post Settings | General | Themes | Widgets | **Posts** | Comments

Who may read posts?

◯ All visitors (no password required)
⦿ Users in the following class(es):
     ✓ Teach42's Class (kidblog.org/teach42scla
     [Add] another Kidblog class URL
◯ Admin/Teacher only
     ☐ Students may read teachers' posts

Post Approval

☐ Admin/Teacher/Moderator must approve posts

Notify these users whenever a post is awaiting approval or published:

☐ teach42 (sdembo@gmail.com)

The first setting defines who will be able to see posts that have been published by your students (a similar setting is available under the Comments menu). The next two settings dictate whether posts will go live immediately or be held for approval and whether you wish to receive notification whenever students save a post.

http://kidblog.org

classroom blogging

Kidblog

🎞 See Kidblog in Action

www.edmodo.com

Make Your Classroom a Community

Social networks have come to play a significant role in our lives. They are a way for us to share information and connect with people around common interests or ideas. Edmodo is one of the first social networks designed exclusively for schools. It takes the concept of a learning management system (LMS) and bakes in rich social interactions, making it a popular choice in classrooms. With a look and feel that is similar to mainstream networks like Facebook, Edmodo is intuitive and incredibly easy to use. What makes Edmodo stand out is the great number of options designed for teachers and students.

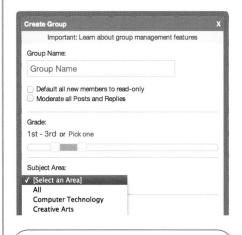

Users can create groups on Edmodo. Members join via a private code.

When teachers sign up for the free service and create a digital class, they are provided a student code for pupils to sign up with. Students enter the code when registering and become a member of their class community. It is worth noting that this eliminates the need for students to provide e-mail addresses or to verify their accounts. They can only create an Edmodo account and join the class community if they have a code provided by their teacher.

Edmodo has developed a uniquely focused social suite of tools for educators. Teachers can post notes, alerts, assignments, quizzes, and polls. Notes are general and can range from a simple statement or question to helpful web resources for students. Edmodo allows teachers to upload files directly (PDFs, PowerPoint

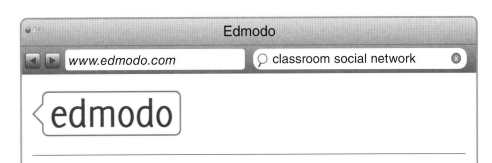

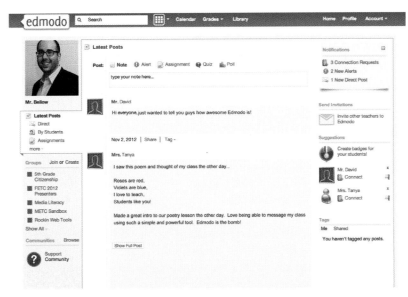

Edmodo often gets compared to Facebook. That's because it's the quintessential social network designed for schools.

docs, etc.) in addition to sharing outside sources via hyperlinks. Teachers can also create alerts, reminding the class about an upcoming event or spreading important news. Alerts appear for the student when they log in to Edmodo or can be broadcast out through e-mails and texts based on their communication preferences. Teachers can create simple quizzes in Edmodo, administering them right through the platform. Even grading can be done (and automated) through the site.

Edmodo lets you broadcast messages to the entire class, specific subgroups, or to individual students. When a teacher creates a poll or quiz, students can respond through the website, the free mobile apps, or even by texting their answers back to Edmodo.

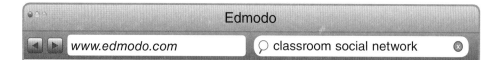

There are a variety of notification options that can be set through the "Settings" menu. You can choose to be notified as each student completes an action, such as sending a note or not being notified at all. Notifications can even be sent directly to a cell phone, allowing you to stay connected to your class at all times if you choose to.

Parent codes are provided as well, allowing them to monitor their students' progress. Parents are able to view a general feed of what is going on in class, including alerts, reminders, and due dates of assignments.

Edmodo launched in late 2008 and has continually added new features. Most recently, it has created an application platform to help teachers guide their students to third-party apps that run within the site. For example, Desmos, which is an amazingly full-featured graphing calculator, can be installed for students and accessed without ever leaving Edmodo. Students don't need to create a separate log-in for these tools and can easily share content through the class discussion group.

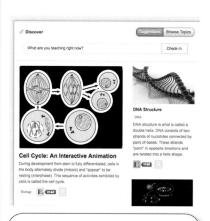

Edmodo's "Discover" feature lets educators share what they are teaching and see related users and resources.

Edmodo was designed with students and teachers in mind and provides an interface that is both intuitive and familiar. Considering its robust feature set, Edmodo is an excellent choice for creating a social network for your students.

Classroom Idea—
Profile Imposter

One idea that has become popular in recent years is to create a social network profile for characters that the class is studying, whether they be fictional or historical. Imagine creating the Edmodo

www.edmodo.com　　　　　○ classroom social network

social network profile of Abraham Lincoln or Atticus Finch. Students are assigned characters to emulate and tasked to respond to prompts that you put up. For example, imagine students are asked to role-play people from the Civil War and are debating both sides of key issues. They can even respond in character to your posts about skirmishes, victories, and defeats.

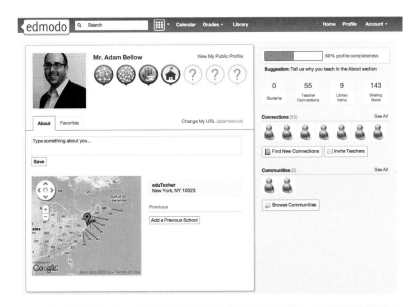

Edmodo allows teachers and students to share their profiles. It also serves as a trophy case to display the badges they earn.

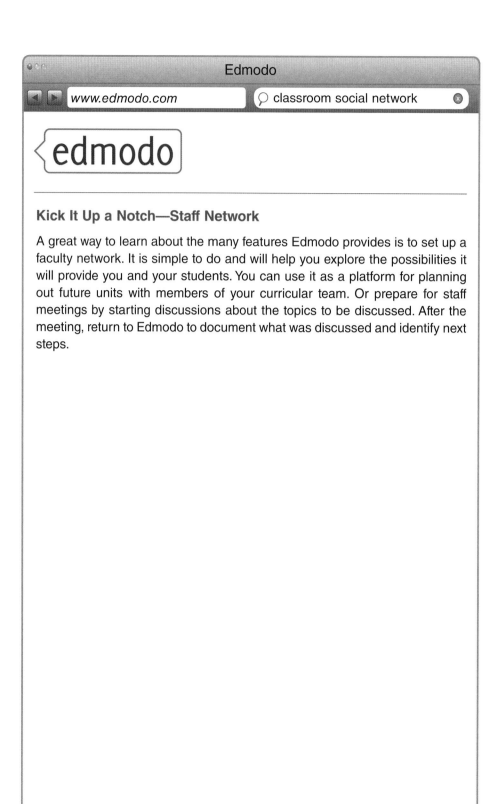

Kick It Up a Notch—Staff Network

A great way to learn about the many features Edmodo provides is to set up a faculty network. It is simple to do and will help you explore the possibilities it will provide you and your students. You can use it as a platform for planning out future units with members of your curricular team. Or prepare for staff meetings by starting discussions about the topics to be discussed. After the meeting, return to Edmodo to document what was discussed and identify next steps.

www.edmodo.com  classroom social network

edmodo

Tweet Tweet: What Fellow Educators Are Saying

> Edmodo has become my digital classroom . . . a place to house the connections between home and school. Whether it be a video to reinforce a concept taught, a discussion we needed more time for, or to check in with my students after hours, Edmodo is a constant within our classroom community.

Jennifer Bond (@teambond)

> Edmodo gives students the chance to experience social networking in a completely safe environment. My own son told me all about it last night. He's not normally into school work, but Edmodo got his attention, "It's just like Facebook, Mom. You should see it!"

Amy Mayer (@friEdTechnology)

> Edmodo is incredible. It allows communication among teachers and students, online discussions, help sessions, posting of resources and is easy to use and free. An essential tool for all educators and students.

David Andrade (@daveandcori)

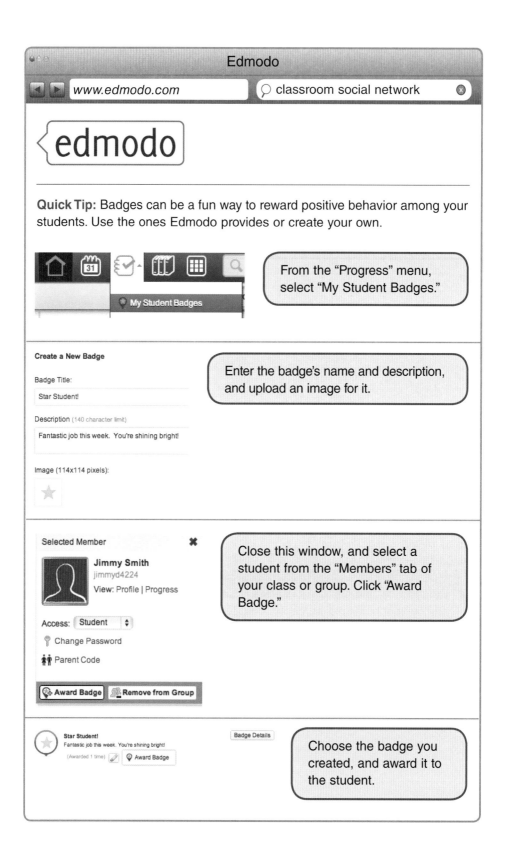

Edmodo

www.edmodo.com — classroom social network

edmodo

Quick Tip: Badges can be a fun way to reward positive behavior among your students. Use the ones Edmodo provides or create your own.

From the "Progress" menu, select "My Student Badges."

Create a New Badge

Badge Title:

Star Student!

Description (140 character limit)

Fantastic job this week. You're shining bright!

Image (114x114 pixels):

Enter the badge's name and description, and upload an image for it.

Selected Member

Jimmy Smith
jimmyd4224
View: Profile | Progress

Access: Student

Change Password

Parent Code

Award Badge   Remove from Group

Close this window, and select a student from the "Members" tab of your class or group. Click "Award Badge."

Star Student!
Fantastic job this week. You're shining bright!
(Awarded 1 time)   Award Badge

Badge Details

Choose the badge you created, and award it to the student.

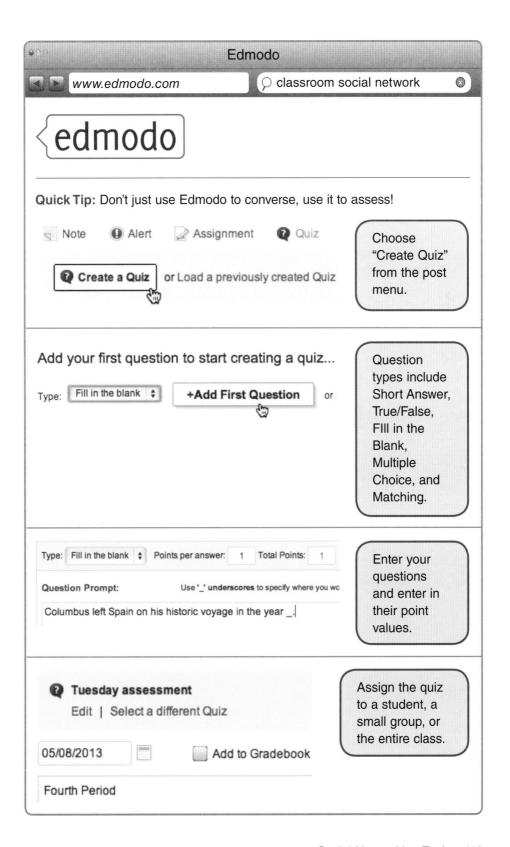

Edmodo

www.edmodo.com   ○ classroom social network ⊗

edmodo

Quick Tip: Don't just use Edmodo to converse, use it to assess!

🗋 Note   ❶ Alert   🖉 Assignment   ❓ Quiz

❓ **Create a Quiz**   or Load a previously created Quiz

> Choose "Create Quiz" from the post menu.

Add your first question to start creating a quiz...

Type: [Fill in the blank ⇕]   **+Add First Question**   or

> Question types include Short Answer, True/False, FIll in the Blank, Multiple Choice, and Matching.

Type: [Fill in the blank ⇕] Points per answer: [1] Total Points: [1]

Question Prompt: Use '_' **underscores** to specify where you wo

Columbus left Spain on his historic voyage in the year _.

> Enter your questions and enter in their point values.

❓ **Tuesday assessment**
   Edit | Select a different Quiz

[05/08/2013] 🗓   ☐ Add to Gradebook

Fourth Period

> Assign the quiz to a student, a small group, or the entire class.

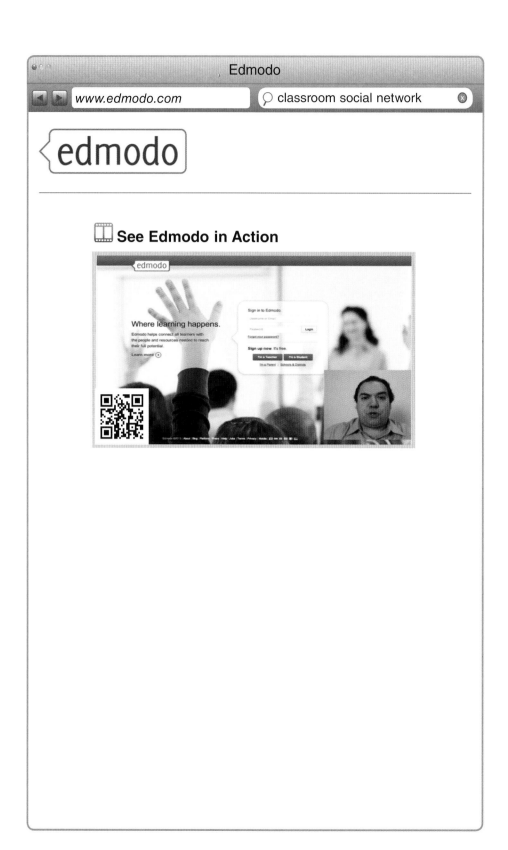

Edmodo

www.edmodo.com | classroom social network

See Edmodo in Action

http://twitter.com/ social network

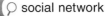

Find out what's happening, right now, with the people and organizations you care about.

There are few websites that have fundamentally changed the way our society communicates as much as Twitter. At the most basic level, it was intended to be a site for people to share what they are doing using 140 characters or less. The number was not arbitrary. An SMS (short message service) message, or text message, can be only 160 characters. They chose 140 to allow enough room to include a username and a brief command along with the message. Twitter was intended to be used primarily as a means of communicating via cell phone, and in particular, via text message. It quickly evolved to encompass far more than just that.

Posting a tweet is simple. Type a message, and make sure you use no more than the allotted 140 characters.

Most social networks require a *handshake* between friends. I send you a friend request. You accept, and we are now connected. Twitter veered away from that model, establishing an environment where I post messages and anybody can choose to *follow* me. It's much more closely aligned to blogging, where authors post content to the world and individuals choose whether they want to subscribe or not. This is why it is often referred to as a microblog. However, the character restriction had a profound effect on the way people used it to communicate.

Twitter is used socially to provide light touches between people, micro-updates that previously may never have been worthy of sharing. While Facebook was providing similar functionality, it is more immersive, requiring more profile information and mutual connections between people. Twitter provided an avenue for people to share and be discovered in a less obtrusive way. Like most social networks, the majority of people began using it for

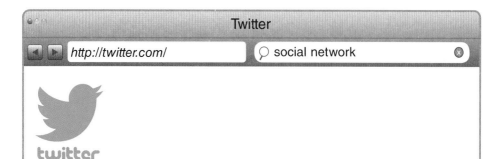

http://twitter.com/   social network

personal reasons at first. Educational uses quickly followed though, and it became a popular way to share professional development resources and integration ideas and to communicate successes and failures with like-minded colleagues.

Today, there are hundreds of thousands of educators collaborating on Twitter, yet it can still be a lonely experience at first. When you first sign up, you are not **following** anyone, and there isn't anyone following you. This means that you may not see any information being shared by anyone that is relevant to you, and when you post a comment, the odds of someone responding are nearly nonexistent. It is critical that new users do a few simple things to set themselves up for success.

Twitter provides only a few profile fields that others are able to see. These include name, username, profile picture (avatar), and a brief bio. If a profile photo is not shared, a generic picture is used. A blank profile and generic avatar is typically viewed as a sign that the person isn't *dedicated* to being active on Twitter. This discourages people from following them. This can create a self-fulfilling prophecy. Users who don't fill in their full info because they are testing out Twitter may find that they have a subpar experience, namely because nobody will take them seriously enough to follow or respond!

Once the profile is established, the user should begin following others. There are several ways to find the right people to follow, but one of the easiest is to simply search for a topic that is interesting to them and follow the people that come up. For example, searching "kindergarten" will return both people who have that word in their profile as well as people who have sent tweets with

Steve Dembo
@teach42   FOLLOWS YOU
Director of Soc Media & Online Community, Discovery Education.
STAR Discovery Educator, Adjunct Professor @ Wilkes U & proud
member of the Eduverse! #GeekPride
Chicago, IL   http://teach42.com

 Following

16,085 TWEETS

1,587 FOLLOWING

13,166 FOLLOWERS

Clicking on a member's profile lets you learn a little about them, including who they follow and who follows them.

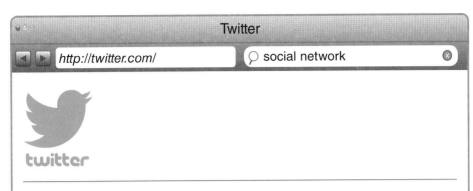

that word recently. Every time you follow someone, they are notified and will have the opportunity to reciprocate. Having a complete profile and personalized avatar will increase the chances that they will do so.

There are three basic types of Twitter messages. Sending out a general message is called a tweet and will be displayed to anybody who is following you. If you include a specific username preceded by an @ symbol (e.g., @adambellow), it is considered to be a reply. Replies are posted publicly to your followers, but the specified user will receive notification that you directed a message to them. The third type of tweet is a **direct message** (DM). In order to send a DM to a person, they must be following you. DMs are private and will only be seen by the person they have been sent to. Many people are initially shy about using the reply feature, believing they may be bothering the user, especially if they have never met them before. On the contrary, that is simply a part of the Twitter ecosystem. Replying to someone's tweet is not only an effective way of jumping into a conversation but it also serves as a passive virtual introduction.

Everyone's tweets are added to the "Twitter stream," which can get pretty crowded when there are over 150 million members who are registered and sending messages. Searching for the content that you want to find is easier than you think. There is a universal search tool that allows you to enter a **hashtag,** a word preceded with a "#" before it. This identifies it as a tag designed to help users find messages related to a specific person, group, or interest. Even without signing in to Twitter, you can search for content that you are interested in. Typing in "#NASA" will bring up all the recent updates about the space program.

One of the most popular education hashtags is #EdChat. #EdChat is more than just a tag that people add to their tweets related to education, it also represents an online conversation taking place every Tuesday. Proposed topics are posted and voted on, and then educators spend time tweeting their thoughts about the topic. #EdChat was founded in 2009 and is one of the oldest and most well-known education hashtags. Tom Whitby, Shelly Terrell, and Steven Anderson founded the event that brings together hundreds of

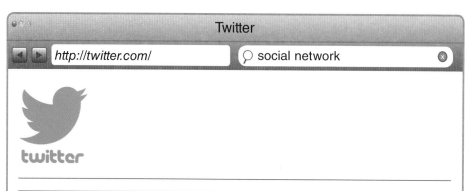

> The main column is your Twitter stream, containing all the tweets from the people you follow.

educators every week. #EdChat has become so popular that it added a second session, taking place seven hours earlier to allow a more diverse global audience to get in on the action.

Perhaps one of the most valuable components of Twitter is the people who fill the network with valuable ideas and resources—not just their content but the actual people behind those short messages. A phenomenon that has taken hold in the past few years is the idea of a **tweet-up.** A tweet-up is when a group of people who use Twitter get together to connect in person. This is a common event at many education and technology conferences, such as ISTE and ASCD.

Twitter also provides educators an excellent means for developing a personal learning network (PLN). These networks provide a place to ask other

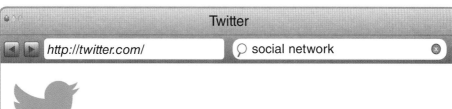

educators around the world how they have tackled classroom issues, whether they be complex or simple. They provide inspiration when it comes to developing new units and advice regarding how to deal with a difficult student, parent, or even a colleague. Given the fact that there are so many active educators on Twitter from diverse backgrounds, users who develop and cultivate their network have a powerful resource at their disposal.

Classroom Idea—Butterfly Tweets

Many classes order caterpillars for the classroom in order to allow students to watch the life cycle of a butterfly. When the caterpillars arrive, allow the students to name them and create a corresponding account on Twitter. Take a digital photo of the caterpillar to use as an avatar, and guide the students in creating an appropriate bio. Keep the jar near a computer, and encourage students to make observations about the caterpillars. Every day, select a student to tweet on behalf of the caterpillars, sharing first person messages based on what the student sees them doing. As they create their chrysalises and hatch into butterflies, encourage the students to document their lives as if the insect were writing the tweets. Whenever the butterfly changes form, be sure to adjust their bio and avatar appropriately. Upon release, the tweets can be saved and aligned with digital photos to create a class journal about the butterfly—through its own eyes. This can also be done with any other class pet, but is well suited to butterflies because of the physical changes they go through.

Kick It Up a Notch—Little Apps, Big Help

As you can imagine, once you get into Twitter, it can be pretty addictive. It's all that access to smart people around the globe who are constantly producing and sharing content. But how do you keep track of it all? Once you have dipped your toes in the water and are ready to really make the most of Twitter, you can set up a dashboard on one of the tools that helps you see more than one Twitter stream at a time. At the moment, the most popular choice is TweetDeck. In a nutshell, it lets you set up multiple searches for either terms or hashtags and view the results in separate columns. You can view a filtered

list of just #EdChat tweets, while the next column over has a filtered list containing tweets on other topics, such as #mobilelearning. Watching one active stream can be overwhelming to some, so it may seem crazy to suggest that having five or ten concurrent streams simplifies things. The key is restricting the information flow. Being able to separate conversations and lists into columns makes it easier to follow a specific conversation.

Other advanced features include the ability to manage more than one Twitter profile without logging in and out. That means that you can be logged into a personal account at the same time as any school accounts you have established.

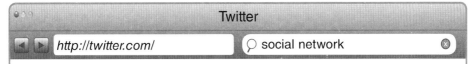

http://twitter.com/

social network

Tweet Tweet: What Fellow Educators Are Saying

Twitter has quickly become the go to, 24/7 tool to acquire resources, knowledge, feedback, ideas, and strategies. It also provides the means to connect with experts, discuss education issues, and track conferences.

Eric Sheninger (@NMHS_Principal)

If you're not supporting your students in using Twitter, you're cheating them out of what is among the most useful tools available for learning with and from a powerful network.

Lisa Nielsen (@InnovativeEdu)

Twitter gives me access to a world of ideas I would never otherwise know existed. It gets me out of the "echo chamber" of my department and into a collection of diverse ideas that inform practice, suggest resources, and inspire me to work in new and innovative ways.

Will Rice (@wrice1978)

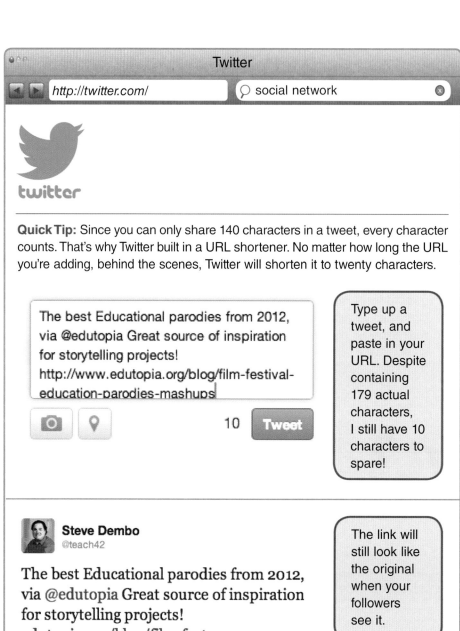

Twitter

http://twitter.com/   🔍 social network   ⊗

twitter

Quick Tip: Since you can only share 140 characters in a tweet, every character counts. That's why Twitter built in a URL shortener. No matter how long the URL you're adding, behind the scenes, Twitter will shorten it to twenty characters.

The best Educational parodies from 2012, via @edutopia Great source of inspiration for storytelling projects! http://www.edutopia.org/blog/film-festival-education-parodies-mashups

📷 📍   10   **Tweet**

Type up a tweet, and paste in your URL. Despite containing 179 actual characters, I still have 10 characters to spare!

Steve Dembo
@teach42

The best Educational parodies from 2012, via @edutopia Great source of inspiration for storytelling projects! edutopia.org/blog/film-fest...

The link will still look like the original when your followers see it.

Twitter

http://twitter.com/ | social network

See Twitter in Action

Visit the online community at www.untanglingthewebcommunity.com.

5

THE BEST OF THE REST

A Grab Bag of Incredible Tools for Schools

When we began writing this book, we decided to start by listing all of the web tools we were fans of with the intention of eliminating options until we had a concise list of our top twenty. The initial list was long—not just grocery-list long, but more like *War and Peace* long. It is astonishing just how many tools are out there—with more being added every day. It forced us to eliminate some incredibly useful and relevant options, solely because we didn't have the space for them in this volume (hint, hint).

The other challenge presented by having such a diverse list of options to choose from was classifying them. While most sites fit neatly into genres, others broke new ground and defied categorization. We bundled what we could, but some fantastic sites represented genres that we didn't have the space to fill out completely. Hence, we decided to simply call this chapter "The Best of the Rest." We're willing to live with the ambiguity of it and hope you will, too.

A decade ago, the technology tools most educators had access to were finite in number, limited primarily by budgets and access. Today, the options available to educators may not be infinite, but they are numerous enough to lend validity to the exaggeration. This is why so many people feel as though they are in a state of perpetual information overload. They immerse themselves in technology, feel like they have a handle on it, and then learn about a site that everyone else has been talking about *forever* (aka a few weeks). It leads to a sense of helplessness, the feeling of always being behind the times. As an individual, this may be discouraging until you realize that we ALL feel that way, the authors of this book included. If you exercise the option to sleep at night, there will always be developments that you are not aware of.

The key to eliminating these discouraging feelings of falling behind is to make peace with one of the tenants of EdTech; so long as you are learning, you are never actually falling behind. Considering the large number of web tools available, it is not unusual for a user not to be aware of what others consider a classic. Wordle, the tool we lead this chapter off with, is a perfect example of this. Among the greater EdTech community, it is a veritable *golden oldie.* And yet many of you reading right now may have never heard of it. Even if you have, you may have never created one yourself. That's not a bad thing or a good thing. It's simply reality. A classic site for one user may be brand new to another. At the end of the day, the big question isn't how *new* a site is but how relevant it is to teachers and students today.

When we shared with people that we were including Wordle, some asked us why we chose it over alternatives like Tagxedo, WordSift, or any of the sites that can also create word clouds. We could have. With every site we included, there were numerous other options that were available. The ones we chose to include were either our personal favorites, iconic enough to define the genre, or were the sites that we felt were relevant to the largest number of educators. There may be sites that have more features, but sometimes the optimal tool isn't defined by the number of bells and whistles—rather by the best user experience.

In the previous chapters, the sites we shared provided a variety of options to achieve a core set of results. In this chapter, we've attempted to share sites that are representative of their genre or in some cases (such as ClassDojo) are simply peerless. These tools may be rather diverse but do share one common thread: They are all excellent choices to enhance classroom experiences for you and your students.

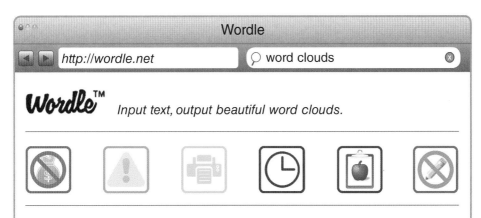

Wordle

http://wordle.net — word clouds

Wordle™ *Input text, output beautiful word clouds.*

Wordle is considered by many to be a prototypical Web 2.0 site. It has astonishingly few features, yet it is robust enough to be used by any educator teaching any subject. It's also incredibly simple.

There are only three steps to generating a Wordle: (1) Click "Create," (2) Paste text, and (3) Click "Go." That's it. Every word from that text field is arranged into an attractive-looking cloud—the most frequently used words appearing largest. At a glance, one can see which words occurred with the highest frequency, providing a means to discern primary themes at a glance even from lengthy passages of text. Color scheme, layout, and font can all be controlled through drop-down menus, allowing users to customize the final product to their individual tastes.

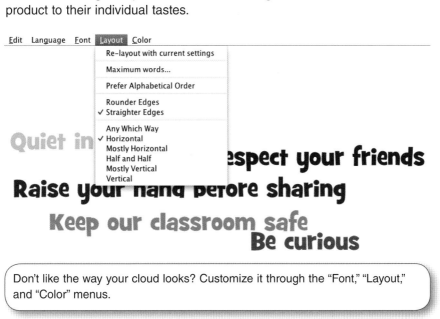

Don't like the way your cloud looks? Customize it through the "Font," "Layout," and "Color" menus.

For such a simple tool, the diversity of ways it is being used by educators is incredible. It can take any block of text and turn it into something that is attractive enough to hang on walls or put on T-shirts. Many teachers take their

Wordle™

class lists and turn them into a word cloud that they print and hang on the door. Librarians create word clouds containing titles of new books that have been added to the shelves. From spelling lists, to classroom rules, educators are using Wordle to make ordinary words into art.

However, when it is used to enhance the curriculum, Wordle really shines. A classic example of this is using it to extract meaning from speeches and written works. By taking a State of the Union address and running it through Wordle, one is able to identify what points the president feels are most important to communicate. By comparing doing this for several presidents, one is able to identify the primary themes of a decade or era. Similarly, one can compare word clouds generated from newspaper articles and blog posts about an identical topic to bring inherent biases to the surface.

www.projectsbyjen.com/GTW

Jen Wagner hosts a "guess the Wordle" challenge each day. Can you figure out the theme of this one?

Classroom Idea—Farewell, Crutch Words

Upon completing the rough draft of a paper or essay, have students highlight the text and create a Wordle from it. Have students print out the word cloud and circle the three words that appear largest. Those are the words that appear most frequently in their work . . . and are now the words that are forbidden to appear in their final draft. During rewrites, students must expand

Wordle

http://wordle.net

word clouds

Wordle™

Paste in a bunch of text:

Raise~your~hand~before~sharing
Respect~your~friends
Quiet~in~the~halls
Keep~our~classroom~safe
Be~curious

> Add a tilde between the words in a phrase to keep them together.

their vocabulary and find new ways to express themselves without relying on "crutch" words.

Kick It Up a Notch— Wordle Secrets

There are several hidden features within Wordle that you can use to exercise far greater control over your word clouds. For example, tie words together by replacing the space between them with a tilde (~). When you click "Create," all tildes will be replaced by spaces, but the words will be kept together as a phrase. This is a great way to ensure that first and last names are retained when creating signs for the classroom.

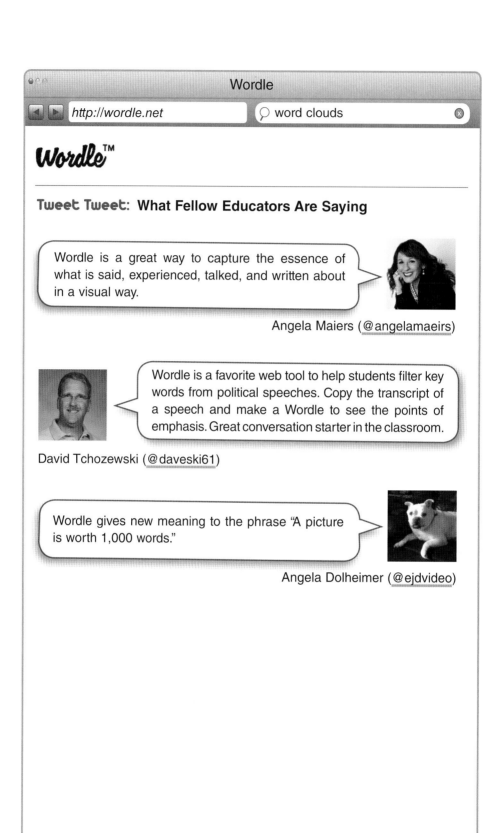

Wordle™

Tweet Tweet: **What Fellow Educators Are Saying**

Wordle is a great way to capture the essence of what is said, experienced, talked, and written about in a visual way.

Angela Maiers (@angelamaeirs)

Wordle is a favorite web tool to help students filter key words from political speeches. Copy the transcript of a speech and make a Wordle to see the points of emphasis. Great conversation starter in the classroom.

David Tchozewski (@daveski61)

Wordle gives new meaning to the phrase "A picture is worth 1,000 words."

Angela Dolheimer (@ejdvideo)

Wordle™

Quick Tip: Remove words from a Wordle without starting over. Right-click (option-click on the Mac) on a specific word, and you can remove it from the cloud.

 **See Wordle in Action**

www.padlet.com   🔍 collaborative brainstorming   ⊗

padlet   *Not just sticky notes on a wall, digital multimedia sticky notes on a wall!*

Sometimes the best tools are the simplest, and <u>Padlet</u> adheres closely to this idea. If you've ever done a brainstorming activity that involved putting sticky notes on a wall, then you already have a good understanding of what Padlet has to offer. There are a few twists that make it even more compelling for use in the classroom.

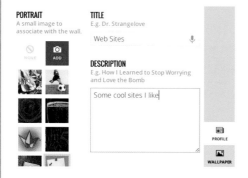

Padlet keeps it simple. A "Title," "Description," and "Portrait" (icon) is all you need to get started.

Padlet provides you an expansive digital canvas with the ability to post an unlimited number of digital notes, each containing a small amount of text (160 characters). That may not seem like much, but just below the text field there's space to insert a URL. That's where the magic starts to kick in. Add a link to an image, and a thumbnail of that picture will appear with the note. Add a link to audio or a video, and a player will be inserted. If you put in a link to a website, then a preview of that site will appear. And with each of these options, clicking through will pull up a window showing the full-sized image, audio, video, or a live view of the website itself! This feature in itself takes Padlet from a simple notes-on-a-wall app to a multimedia experience with incredible classroom potential.

Another feature that makes the site so appealing to educators is that walls can be both interactive and collaborative. Visitors can not only rearrange the notes on the wall but they can add their own (depending on the settings, of course). This makes it a great site for aggregating ideas as well as information. While it may lack the ability to connect notes like you would in a mind map,

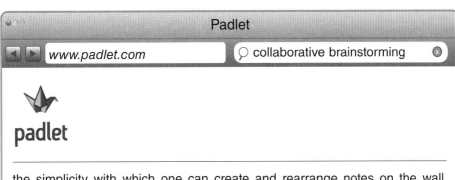

the simplicity with which one can create and rearrange notes on the wall makes it compelling for group brainstorms and collaborative note-taking.

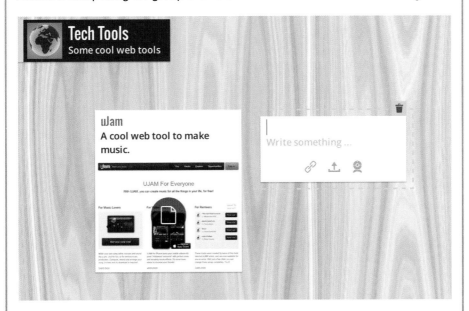

Notes can contain much more than just text. Try adding images, links, or videos to a note.

There is no registration required to get started. From the main page, click on "Build a Wall" and you can dive right in. You can even share the wall with others and let them collaborate with you. However, if you do not choose to log in and save it to an account, you will be unable to make changes to your wall after twenty-four hours. Registering for the site allows you to save your walls, set up notifications, and make use of the moderation features.

While you can create a wall with a single click, there are several options that you will want to fill in. You can customize your page by choosing an avatar image, title, subtitle, and background. Wall-specific preferences include making it public or private, deciding who has permission to post (everyone or only

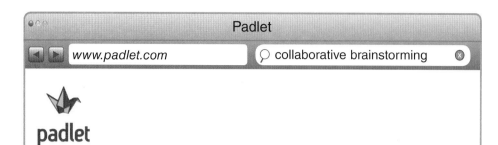

yourself), and determining whether you want to moderate posts before they go live. Finally, you need to choose a URL for your wall, an address that people will use to find it. While this may be optional, choosing a friendly name makes it much easier to share your wall with others. The address will be http://padlet .com/wall/WhatEverYouTypeHere.

Regarding the public or private preference, one of the things that makes Padlet so friendly to educators is that there is no public directory of walls or a way to search through other people's creations. When you create a wall, the only people who can get to it are people *you* give the URL to. There's no worries about it showing up in Google unless you embed it into a blog and share it yourself. When you set a wall to private, nobody can get to it unless they are logged in to your account. If you set it to public, nobody can get to it unless they have been given the URL by you. Essentially, it's hidden in plain sight. In this way, even though walls may be public, random strangers won't be able to stumble upon the work that you and your students are doing together.

Padlet has added some interesting new ways to view the information saved within it. Under "Layout," users can switch from the traditional wall style to "Stream," which displays the notes linearly, as you might find on a blog. They have also included the ability to save walls offline in both PDF and Excel formats.

Classroom Idea—Mix and Match the Animals

Animal classification can be an esoteric concept to introduce to students because the characteristics may seem arbitrary at first. Padlet can be a great way to provide a visual demonstration of the different ways to classify animals, allowing students to explore the idea openly before introducing them to the scientific classes.

Begin by creating a wall with a large variety of animals including mammals, fish, birds, reptiles, and amphibians. Depending on the age of the students, this can be done ahead of time by the teacher or by having students add their own notes to the wall. Each note should have the name of the animal along with a picture of that animal. Direct the students to analyze the animals and to put them into groups. After arranging the animals in groups, have the students discuss what characteristics they keyed in on to organize the

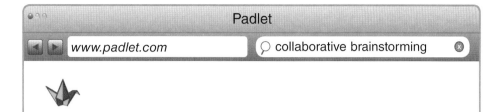

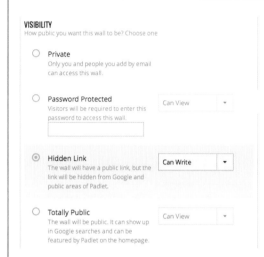

VISIBILITY
How public you want this wall to be? Choose one

○ Private
Only you and people you add by email can access this wall.

○ Password Protected
Visitors will be required to enter this password to access this wall.

◉ Hidden Link
The wall will have a public link, but the link will be hidden from Google and public areas of Padlet.

○ Totally Public
The wall will be public. It can show up in Google searches and can be featured by Padlet on the homepage.

Can View ▾

Can Write ▾

Can View ▾

Use the Visibility panel to make your walls as public or as private as you like. Choose "Yes" for "Moderate Posts?" so posts require your approval before new content goes live (aka the middle school feature).

animals in that way. Then reset the wall and do it again. See how many different ways the students can organize the same group of animals, each time discussing what characteristics they used to classify them. By color? By skin type? By size? By method of transportation? If students are doing this individually, they can print out their arrangements before refreshing the screen to save their creations.

After allowing the students ample time to explore these ideas, identify the proper classifications and what the characteristics are of each. Start with a single class, such as reptiles, and have the students pull out all the animals that qualify. Continue doing this until all the animals have been classified, and then save the results.

Kick It Up a Notch—Start With the K and W and Return for the L

When introducing a new unit, many teachers employ the KWL technique. They start off documenting what the students *know* (or think they know) about a topic, expand that to what they *want* to know, and then come back at the end to see what they've *learned.*

During the opening discussion, create a new sticky note for each idea the students have about what they know and want to know. Rearrange the notes as needed, to demonstrate where ideas overlap or are similar enough

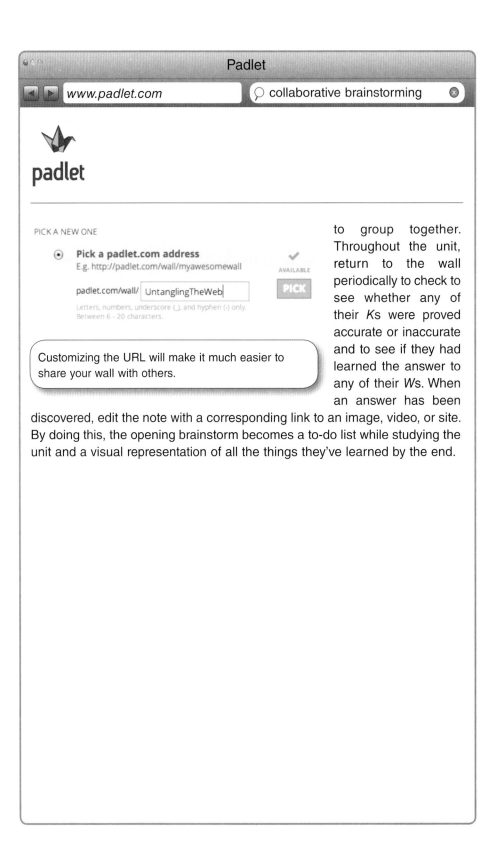

to group together. Throughout the unit, return to the wall periodically to check to see whether any of their *K*s were proved accurate or inaccurate and to see if they had learned the answer to any of their *W*s. When an answer has been discovered, edit the note with a corresponding link to an image, video, or site. By doing this, the opening brainstorm becomes a to-do list while studying the unit and a visual representation of all the things they've learned by the end.

www.padlet.com 〈 collaborative brainstorming ⊗

padlet

Tweet Tweet: What Fellow Educators Are Saying

> During National School Board Week, Padlet was the perfect way for the students on my campus to show our school board members how much we appreciate them. It was more creative than the traditional "form" letters the students had written in the past, and was an avenue for instructing our school board about the use of Web 2.0 tools in the classroom.

Karen Wells (@karenwells)

> The day or two before an assessment I set up a "wall" for students to post last minute questions, things they need clarified, etc. I check in and respond but the best part is the kids' responses. They take ownership of our class learning community and answer each others' queries.

Adrienne F. Norris (@adriennenorris)

> Padlet is a fantastic site for students to brainstorm thoughts and ideas collaboratively. We've had 4th graders pick a topic, research, and create a fact wall.

Dennis Grice (@dgrice)

www.padlet.com | collaborative brainstorming

padlet

Quick Tip: If you want your wall to be collaborative but are still concerned about notes going live without seeing them first, be sure to use the moderation feature (middle school teachers, pay attention to this one).

Old Glory
William Driver named *his* flag Old Glory, but it has since become a nickname for **all** American flags

REMOVE   APPROVE

When a student adds a new post, it will appear on your board with "Remove" and "Approve" buttons.

See Padlet in Action

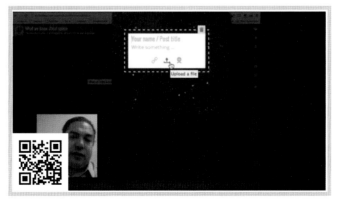

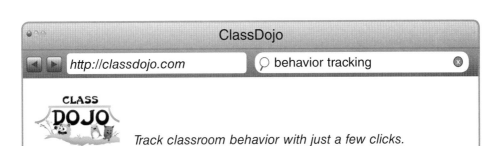

http://classdojo.com   behavior tracking

Track classroom behavior with just a few clicks.

Every once in a while, a new site comes along that is so simple and yet so useful that it seems astonishing it hadn't been invented already. All that ClassDojo does is help teachers track student behaviors. That's it. Seems almost too obvious, doesn't it? After all, there are hundreds of ways to do that already. The reason ClassDojo stands out is that it has removed as many barriers to the logging process as possible. Essentially, they've eliminated *clicks*. Once the class and behaviors are set up, teachers can log a behavior for a student with just two taps; tap student name and tap the behavior. Move on with class.

Log behavior two clicks at a time.

All educators know that they should be assessing their students continuously and logging specific behaviors as they see them. Paper-based systems require that the teacher carry a clipboard throughout the day and then enter the data in chunks on a daily or weekly basis. Most digital systems require expensive proprietary software or web-based interfaces that often are not optimized for teachers to use away from the desktop computer. ClassDojo is free, web based, has iOS apps available, and a mobile interface for Android and other platforms. But more than any other reason, educators are flocking to ClassDojo because the actual logging of activity is lightning quick and more convenient than any other system out there.

ClassDojo does require registration but bypasses the confirmation e-mail, enabling users to dive right in. It has a step-by-step demo that begins after registration, taking new users through the process of setting up their first class. After selecting a grade level and name for the class, teachers can begin entering their students' names. The final step involves entering in the

behaviors that they want to track. While the site has several suggestions (e.g., "Creativity," "Participation," "Hard Work"), every behavior is customizable, enabling educators to enter in exactly the criteria that they want to track.

Once the teacher starts the class, a list of all the students appears along with randomly assigned avatars. When the teacher sees a behavior that needs to be logged, she just taps on the student's name and then taps on the behavior that they exhibited. Positive and negative behaviors are separated into two tabs. By default, positive behaviors log a +1 to the student's score, and an encouraging *ding* is heard. Conversely, negative behaviors subtract one point from their score and generate a buzz. While behaviorists may be able to vouch for the effectiveness of the audio feedback, educators who cringe at the crude mechanism can mute the volume or disable it entirely via the site settings. At the end of the class period, tallies are saved for every student individually as well as the group. A comment box is available to add comments to an individual student, and the results can be e-mailed to parents as a PDF.

ClassDojo does more than just behavior tracking; it can also serve as a simple means for logging attendance. One click marks a student as tardy or absent.

ClassDojo has been in a state of rapid development. Just a few months after their public launch, they added the ability for both parents and students to create their own accounts. Students receive codes from their teachers, enabling them to check their own progress as well as customize their avatar. Upon receiving a report from the teacher, parents are able to create their own account, which enables them to see ongoing reports of their student's behaviors along with any teacher commentary.

The real power of this site lies in the user's ability to customize the behaviors being tracked. The same

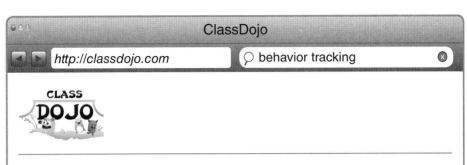

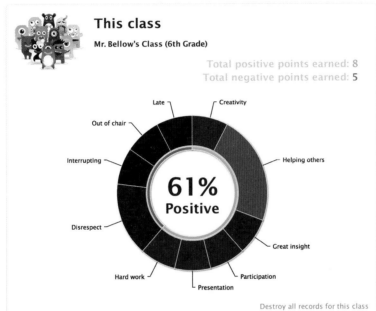

This class

Mr. Bellow's Class (6th Grade)

Total positive points earned: 8
Total negative points earned: 5

Late • Creativity
Out of chair
Interrupting • Helping others

61%
Positive

Disrespect
Great insight

Hard work
Participation
Presentation

Destroy all records for this class

> Don't just assess individual students; use class records to assess the class progress as a whole.

interface kindergarten teachers use to assess phonemic awareness can be used by PE teachers to log fitness accomplishments. Specific behaviors that need to be monitored as part of an IEP can be logged as easily as assessing which students have mastered multiplication tables. ClassDojo has created an ideal way to track students *in the moment* whether the teacher uses a computer, tablet, or mobile device.

Classroom Idea—Day 1: Began Working on Report Cards

For many teachers, the month before report cards are due becomes a period of time spent frantically scrolling through standard after standard, determining the progress each student has made against each criteria. Use ClassDojo to be more proactive! At the beginning of a term, customize the

Don't just track the negative behaviors; positive reinforcement can be an incredibly effective classroom management technique.

behaviors to reflect things you'll need to assess the students on during report card season. As soon as you see a student exhibit mastery of a particular skill, check it off for that student immediately. If you will be using the site as a general behavior tracker as well, create an alternate *hidden* class that you can use for report cards. With two extra taps, you will be far ahead of schedule when it comes time to begin report card evaluations. As an added bonus, you'll have much better records regarding when a student began mastering each skill.

Kick It Up a Notch—Turning the Tables

ClassDojo is an excellent way for you to evaluate your students' behaviors on an ongoing basis. However, if you spin it around, it can also be an excellent way for your students to evaluate . . . you! Create a new class with only one student in it: yourself. Customize the behaviors to include positive criteria like "paused for questions" and "good analogy." You can also add negative criteria like "explanation unclear" and "need more examples." Designate a single student or have the entire class log in to your account, and let them use it to evaluate you throughout a lesson. Not only can this provide you with feedback

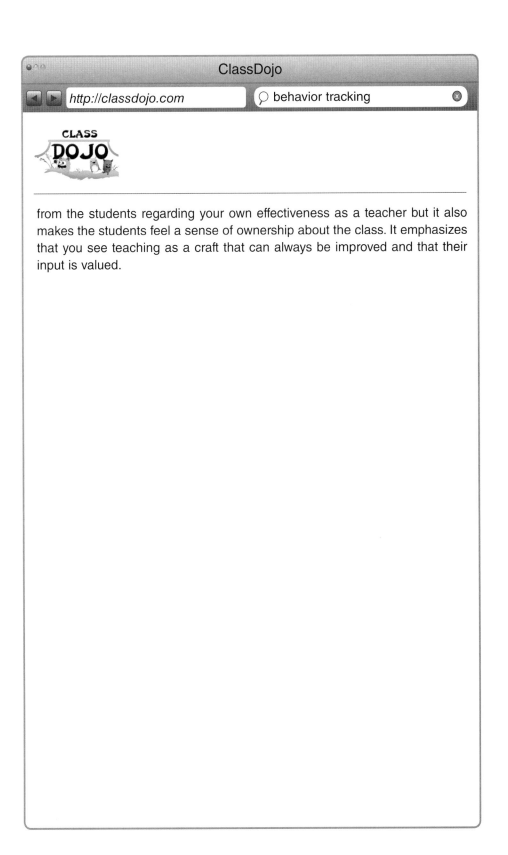

from the students regarding your own effectiveness as a teacher but it also makes the students feel a sense of ownership about the class. It emphasizes that you see teaching as a craft that can always be improved and that their input is valued.

http://classdojo.com   behavior tracking

Tweet Tweet: What Fellow Educators Are Saying

ClassDojo is an excellent tool for classroom management but even better for classroom motivation. Students love seeing their avatars and hearing those positive points being awarded. Great way to give you, your students (and their parents) a snapshot of how class went that day.

Lance Rougeux (@lrougeux)

Our teachers are using Dojo in the classroom to motivate kids for positive behavior and to track any observable learning goal. It has been hugely successful in elementary and middle schools. The site is super easy to use, colorful, and engaging. There is a very low learning curve for teachers. Students love being able to interact with the site with their home accounts.

Amy Boehman-Pollitt (@trtamybp)

ClassDojo cares about how educators use their product, and they truly want to help with focusing on positive choices. They keep adding great reporting functions I think teachers and parents will love.

Diane Main (@dowbiggin)

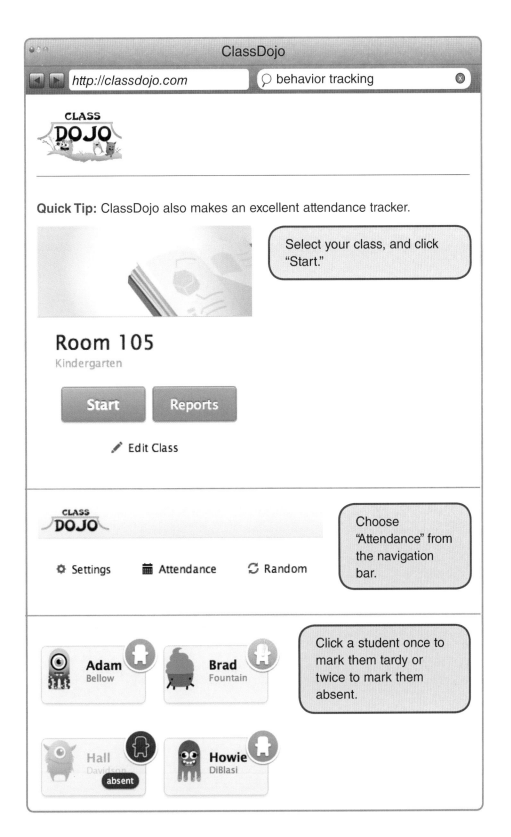

ClassDojo

http://classdojo.com   🔍 behavior tracking   ⊗

Quick Tip: ClassDojo also makes an excellent attendance tracker.

Select your class, and click "Start."

Room 105
Kindergarten

Start   **Reports**

✏ Edit Class

⚙ Settings   📅 Attendance   🔄 Random

Choose "Attendance" from the navigation bar.

Adam Bellow

Brad Fountain

Click a student once to mark them tardy or twice to mark them absent.

Hall Davidson   absent

Howie DiBlasi

http://classdojo.com

behavior tracking

📽 See ClassDojo in Action

Visit the online community at www.untanglingthewebcommunity.com.

6

BONUS SECTION!

Okay, we admit it. We are weak willed and just couldn't resist the chance to throw in a few more. There are literally hundreds of tools that we could have included in this book. Limit it to just twenty? Impossible. That's why we've decided to sneak in a few bonus sites from our personal collection of favorites. Enjoy these fabulous tools on the house, gratis, free of charge.

http://capzles.com   ○ multimedia timelines   ⊗

capzles *Time. Captured.*

Creating a visual timeline or sequence is something that is not new to computing. Software to make timelines has existed for decades—with a variety of titles available for students to use in class. However, Capzles is a refreshingly unique take on timeline creation that goes far beyond what you may have seen previously. Not only is it completely web based but it bakes in a series of enhanced features that make creating and viewing a Capzle both a cool and educationally sound experience. Don't let the word *timeline* confuse you, because these projects are far from a static, linear experience.

> Before creating your own Capzle, explore their highlighted content so you can get a handle on what the possibilities are.

Capzles are interactive experiences. Every point along the line can house a series of multimedia objects, providing a much richer experience than a simple label. A Civil War timeline might have a dozen events listed, each portraying a major event or battle. Each of those points could contain multiple images, PDFs, links, and videos that bring the event to life.

http://capzles.com   multimedia timelines

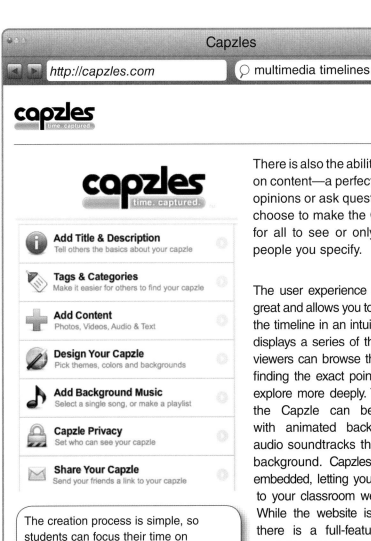

There is also the ability to comment on content—a perfect way to share opinions or ask questions. You can choose to make the Capzle public for all to see or only viewable to people you specify.

The user experience on this site is great and allows you to scroll through the timeline in an intuitive manner. It displays a series of thumbnails that viewers can browse through rapidly, finding the exact point they wish to explore more deeply. The design of the Capzle can be customized with animated backgrounds and audio soundtracks that play in the background. Capzles can also be embedded, letting you publish them to your classroom website or blog. While the website is flash based, there is a full-featured iOS app available, which allows you to create Capzles from your Apple handheld device.

Classroom Idea—What I Did On My Summer Vacation

When most people think of timelines, they think social studies, using them to document a moment in history. But they can also be used to create far more personal projects for students. Instead of a what-I-did-this-summer assignment, have your students create a Capzle documenting their experiences since school closed for the year. They can include text, audio, images, or videos that represent what they want to share with the class. Their project can aggregate a broad overview of the significant events from the summer. More interestingly though, Capzles can be a creative way to tell

a thematic digital story, keying in on one event that takes place over a series of time.

Kick It Up a Notch—Year in Preview

Students aren't the only ones able to use Capzles. One of the more unique uses we've seen is a teacher who creates an interactive syllabus using Capzles. To do this, create a Capzle and add to it an overview of the significant content your class will be studying throughout the year. Add key information about the course, such as the types of things that years ago may have been handed out on flyers the first day of class. Post presentations you will share with the students throughout the year, whether they be PowerPoint files or links to online presentations (like Prezi). Fill in the rest of the timeline with key milestones and important classroom events.

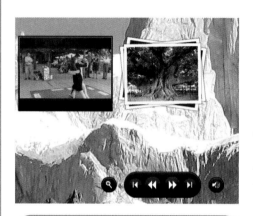

Stacks are represented on the timeline as a pile of images.

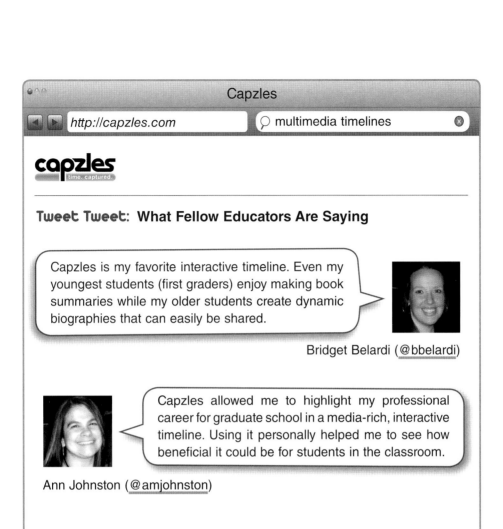

capzles
time. captured.

Tweet Tweet: What Fellow Educators Are Saying

Capzles is my favorite interactive timeline. Even my youngest students (first graders) enjoy making book summaries while my older students create dynamic biographies that can easily be shared.

Bridget Belardi (@bbelardi)

Capzles allowed me to highlight my professional career for graduate school in a media-rich, interactive timeline. Using it personally helped me to see how beneficial it could be for students in the classroom.

Ann Johnston (@amjohnston)

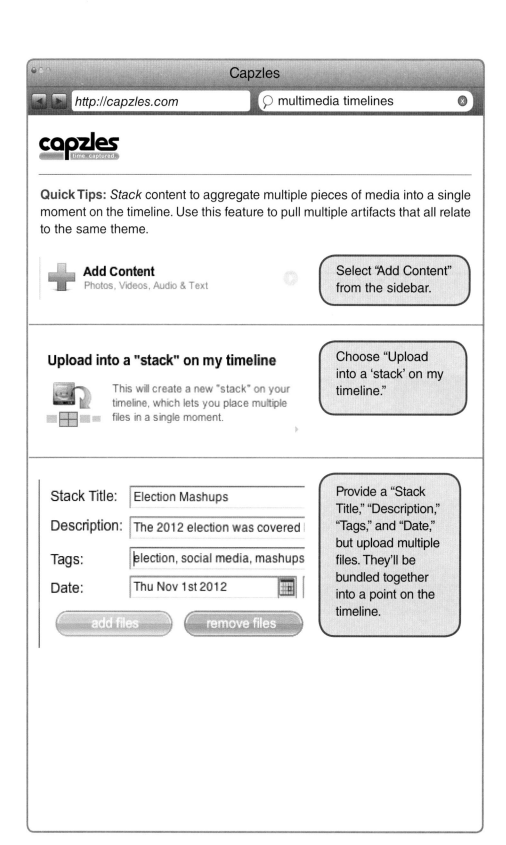

Capzles

http://capzles.com   multimedia timelines ⊗

capzles
time. captured.

Quick Tips: *Stack* content to aggregate multiple pieces of media into a single moment on the timeline. Use this feature to pull multiple artifacts that all relate to the same theme.

Add Content
Photos, Videos, Audio & Text

> Select "Add Content" from the sidebar.

Upload into a "stack" on my timeline

This will create a new "stack" on your timeline, which lets you place multiple files in a single moment.

> Choose "Upload into a 'stack' on my timeline."

Stack Title: Election Mashups

Description: The 2012 election was covered

Tags: election, social media, mashups

Date: Thu Nov 1st 2012

add files   remove files

> Provide a "Stack Title," "Description," "Tags," and "Date," but upload multiple files. They'll be bundled together into a point on the timeline.

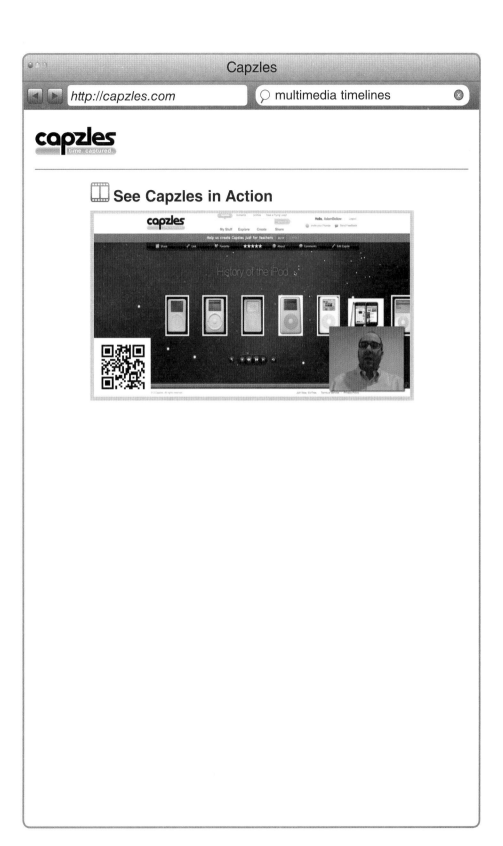

See Capzles in Action

 easelly *The infographic generator that you were always looking for.*

Infographics have become an extremely popular way to share visual representations of data sets. Research and statistics, often from a variety of sources, are aggregated together and shared through a visual theme. They are simple to view and digest but more complex to create than most people realize. The graphic design involved in making the graphic look clean, concise, and cohesive requires a sophisticated understanding of design elements that has made the format inaccessible to the average user. There are several sites that advertise the ability to generate infographics, but most revolve around social stats and provide little ability to customize the reports.

Easelly's interface is deceptively simple. There appears to be few options, but it can be used to create sophisticated infographics.

Easelly is one of the only sites that provides an open framework for creating infographics online. It provides ample templates for users to choose from, including frequently used visual themes such as the fifty states, a global map, male vs. female, and social media. Unlike the others, these templates provide

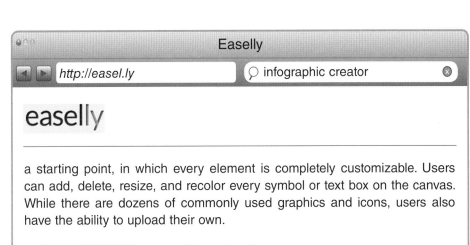

easelly

a starting point, in which every element is completely customizable. Users can add, delete, resize, and recolor every symbol or text box on the canvas. While there are dozens of commonly used graphics and icons, users also have the ability to upload their own.

> Don't forget to explore the categories within the "Objects" menu. There are dozens of graphics within each folder.

The site itself is simple to use, but that doesn't mean it is easy to create an infographic. Determining what data to share, how to represent it, and then creating a visually pleasing product is still a challenging task. Easelly is a design engine, not a data engine. You cannot import data sets and have the site create charts for you. For each set of data, you select the icons you will use and customize them as needed. For example, if you want to display a section depicting that 50 percent of your students are male, you would need to copy and paste ten person icons onto the page and then change the color for half of them. Easelly makes it simple to do so and provides excellent visual cues to ensure that your icons line up straight, but it is still a manual process.

While some may lament that it isn't as automagical a process as they might like, in some ways that makes it even better suited for an educational environment. An infographic is nothing more than another way to share information, much like a PowerPoint presentation or digital story. The heart of it is the content that the creator wants to share with others. Students should be spending the bulk of their time determining what information to present and considering what the proper way to visualize it would be. This process is remarkably similar to storyboarding a movie or creating an outline prior to writing a paper. Once the back end work is complete, then students can log in to Easelly to create their project.

Completed projects can be shared online or saved offline. The site flattens the image and allows users to download it as a JPG. The image can be sent via e-mail, posted to websites, or printed out and displayed. Embed codes

To get you on your way quickly, Easelly provides a variety of vhemes (visual themes) to start from.

are provided for easy sharing via blog, and projects can be marked as public or private.

Easelly is a mixed bag in some ways. While it is the most robust and simple infographic creator available online, it can sometimes be a challenge to get certain elements to look exactly as you might want. For those seeking a professional level graphic design engine, this wouldn't suit the bill. But for teachers and students looking to make use of infographics as a medium for sharing information, Easelly is an excellent solution.

Classroom Idea—Class Census

Have your students create a brief form that they can use to survey each other. Once they have their data in order, have them identify ten interesting things worth sharing. For each of those ten items, encourage them to think about how they could demonstrate the data visually. When they have outlined their ideas, have each student log in to Easelly and create an infographic

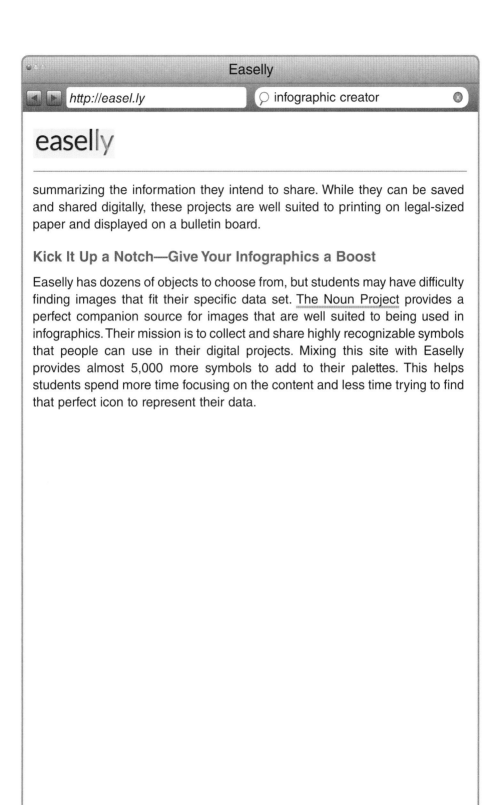

http://easel.ly   infographic creator

easelly

summarizing the information they intend to share. While they can be saved and shared digitally, these projects are well suited to printing on legal-sized paper and displayed on a bulletin board.

Kick It Up a Notch—Give Your Infographics a Boost

Easelly has dozens of objects to choose from, but students may have difficulty finding images that fit their specific data set. The Noun Project provides a perfect companion source for images that are well suited to being used in infographics. Their mission is to collect and share highly recognizable symbols that people can use in their digital projects. Mixing this site with Easelly provides almost 5,000 more symbols to add to their palettes. This helps students spend more time focusing on the content and less time trying to find that perfect icon to represent their data.

easelly

Tweet Tweet: What Fellow Educators Are Saying

Easily the latest, greatest thing to visual learning is the infographic. But infographics themselves are not so easy to create. Enter the free and still in beta site Easelly, which pretty much lives up to its name! With a few slick template choices, text, objects, and shapes to add anyone can create a slick looking free infographic that adds interest, meaning, and comprehension to text-heavy content.

Gwyneth Jones (@gwynethjones)

The name of the site, Easelly, tells you just how easy it is to make infographics! This site provides you with fifteen customizable themes to start with or just a blank slate if you want to start from scratch. The themes are totally customizable and you can edit color, text, icons, size, or background. You can upload your own graphs and images, too.

Kathy Shrock (@kathyschrock)

Easelly is an excellent way to embrace content creation in the classroom. Creating infographics require students to truly interact with the content in meaningful ways, and Easelly turns their efforts into amazing creations.

Sean Junkins (@sjunkins)

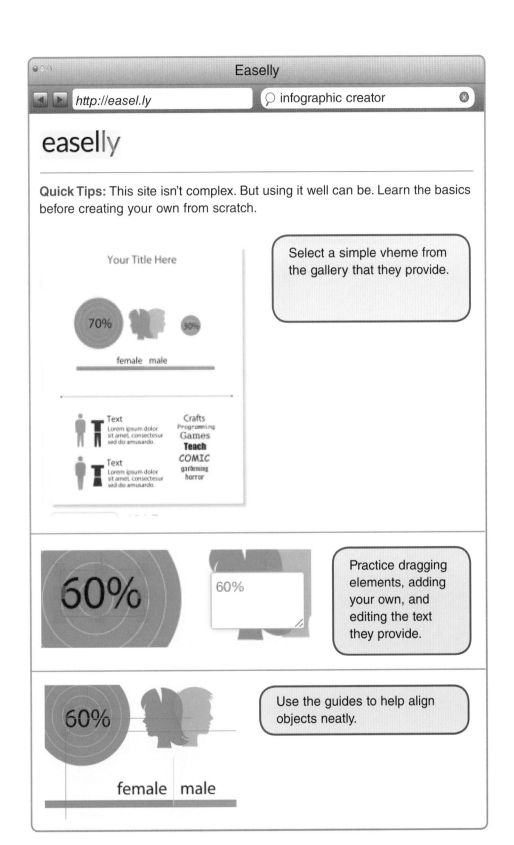

easelly

Quick Tips: This site isn't complex. But using it well can be. Learn the basics before creating your own from scratch.

Select a simple vheme from the gallery that they provide.

Your Title Here

70%   30%

female   male

Text
Lorem ipsum dolor sit amet, consectetur sed do amusardo.

Text
Lorem ipsum dolor sit amet, consectetur sed do amusardo.

Crafts
Programming
Games
Teach
COMIC
gardening
horror

Practice dragging elements, adding your own, and editing the text they provide.

60%

60%

Use the guides to help align objects neatly.

60%

female   male

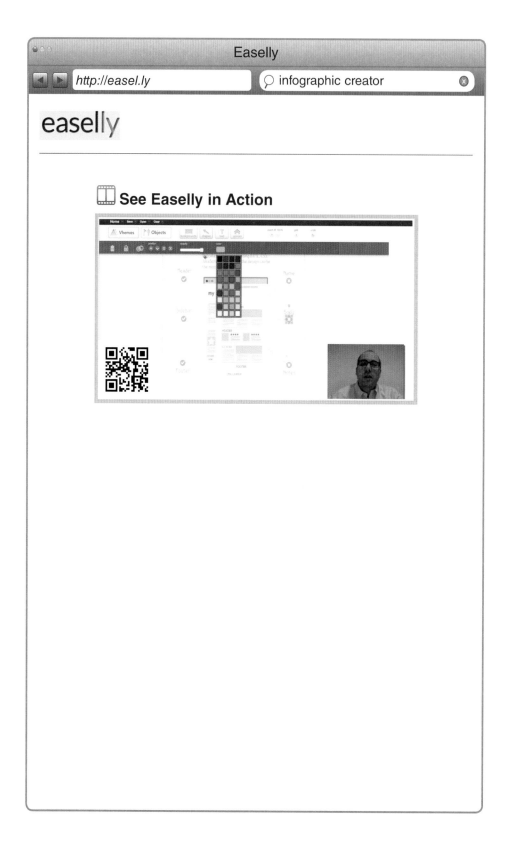

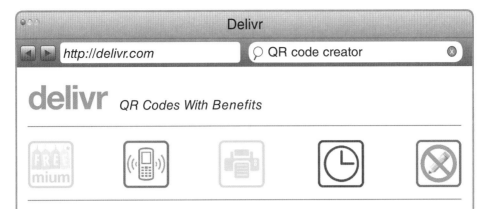

delivr *QR Codes With Benefits*

QR codes have been building in popularity slowly over the past several years but have only recently entered into the mainstream. You've probably seen these small tags popping up on posters, TV advertisements, products at your local store, and in this book! While it may look a bit like a strange alien symbol, a QR code is nothing more than a square barcode that serves as a hyperlink to content on the Internet. Scan the code with a QR reader on a smartphone and you'll instantly be taken to a website. They're appearing with increasing frequency on products and in advertising, but they can also be a powerful tool for teachers and students.

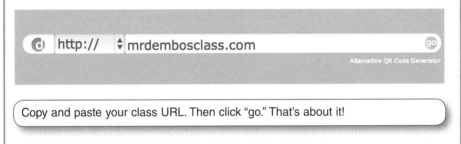

Copy and paste your class URL. Then click "go." That's about it!

Delivr is a site that allows anybody to create a QR code in seconds. Paste in a URL and click "go"; it provides you with a QR code that works instantly. The code itself is nothing more than an image. There's nothing special about the image. You can treat it the same as you would any other digital photo or clip art you find on the Internet. You can save it to your desktop, copy and paste it into a document, print it out, or e-mail it to a colleague. Delivr also provides a shortened URL for people who don't have a smartphone or QR code reader. The site makes it incredibly easy to create and share your first QR code.

There are plenty of sites that allow you to create QR codes, but there are a few features that make Delivr stand out. The first is that if you do choose to register for the site, it will save a list of every QR code you have ever created. At any time, you can browse that list and see how many times people have scanned that specific QR code. If you're a data junkie, you can even plug in your Google Analytics info and get more detailed reports.

delivr

Download as: PNG | JPG | EPS | SVG

QR codes are just image files. Save them to your desktop, or copy and paste them anywhere you can add an image to.

What's even more useful though is that you can choose to edit any QR code you have created, changing the URL that it links to. This may seem like an odd thing to do, but remember that the code itself is nothing more than a shortcut. Think of it like a phone number. If someone were to dial it, your phone would ring. But if you buy a new phone or move, you can have the phone company change it so the same phone number now rings on the new phone. If you print out a QR code and put it up in your classroom, this week it can point people who scan it to your classroom website. Next week, you can go back to Delivr and edit the place that the code points to, sending new scans to a different location. The code itself stays the same, so you don't need to print a new copy. But what changes is the location that it points to. This is a very simple concept, but it opens up some very interesting possibilities.

Best of all, you don't need a smartphone of your own to make use of Delivr. All you need is to be able to type in a URL and click submit, and you're leveraging one of the most cutting-edge technologies of the past several years.

Classroom Idea—Scan Here to Activate Learning

QR codes can be a fantastic way to provide students with a focus activity as they enter the classroom—particularly in schools that have begun shifting to a bring your own device (BYOD) environment. Find an image or video related to something that you are studying that day, and create a QR code pointing to it. Print out the code, and hang it up outside the classroom. As soon as the

delivr

Welcome to Mr. Bellow's Class
Room 42

Add a QR code to the sign on your door, and your geek cred immediately goes up by ten points.

students see it, their natural curiosity will kick into gear. They won't be able to resist scanning it and seeing where it will take them. In this way, before they've even entered the door, you've focused their thoughts and conversations on a topic they'll be studying soon. Every morning, take a minute to visit Delivr, and change the link to point to a new image, video, or website. They'll look forward to scanning the code on the way in to get a sneak peek at what they'll be learning about that day. Not only does this serve as a great activation activity but it also helps classroom management by providing some structure to the arrival process.

Kick It Up a Notch—Adding Digital Layers

While QR codes are fantastic for teachers to use, the real fun begins when you put them in the hands of students. Adding a QR code to a project allows digital content to be layered over any physical artifact. If you are creating dioramas about Greek mythology, students who finish early can add a QR code to their project. This opens up a limitless number of possibilities for extending the assignment. Does the QR code link to a Google Site about the author? Or to their page on the class blog describing how they created the project? Perhaps it links to a video about the myth depicted in the scene or a survey assessing what the viewer thinks about the project? Since it's an extension of the project and not the assignment itself, this element can be entirely student directed.

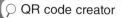

http://delivr.com   ⊙ QR code creator

delivr

Tweet Tweet: What Fellow Educators Are Saying

Delivr is an amazing way to integrate QR codes into your classroom. With Delivr, QR codes are customizable, trackable, and allow students to communicate in a creative and engaging way.

Cate Beck (@catebeck)

I really enjoy using Delivr for quick QR code creation of websites that I am browsing. You can share via Twitter/Facebook or just download the image in JPG or PNG formats to be used in presentations, scavenger hunts, or even virtual information shares.

Dean Mantz (@dmantz7)

I've put QR codes in trees, on the back of bus seats, and handouts. I have not gotten a QR tattoo although others have. The beauty of registering at Delivr is that you can change the QR destination. Pretty critical if you're going the tattoo route. The tracking is nice, too.

Hall Davidson (@halldavidson)

Delivr

http://delivr.com   QR code creator

delivr

Quick Tip: Delivr keeps track of every click and scan. Use the dashboard to see how your QR codes have actually been used.

Views	QR Scans	NFC Taps	
97	**5**	**0**	
views	qr scans	nfc taps	analytics

Log into your dashboard to see details about "Views" and "QR Scans."

Operating System	Views	%
■ Desktop Operating Systems	53	54.6%
■ Other Mobile Operating Systems	27	27.8%
■ Apple iOS (iPad, iPad Mini)	9	9.3%
■ Apple iOS (iPhone, iPod Touch)	6	6.2%
■ BlackBerry OS	2	2.1%

Want more information? Select "analytics," and see far more information, including a breakdown of devices that have scanned it.

See Delivr in Action

CONTINUE THE LEARNING JOURNEY

As you can see, there are so many wonderful web tools that can help engage students, enhance learning, and make your classroom rock! We have just scraped the tip of the iceberg here and hope you will continue your learning journey with us online. Make the most of the resources we've shared by connecting with other readers on the _Untangling the Web_ community site. We'll be watching for you there and can't wait to see where your own explorations lead.

We look forward to learning with you.

GLOSSARY

Avatar—Avatars are images that users select to represent them on a social networking site. Avatars can be photographs or any other image that a user feels expresses himself.

Back Channel—A back channel refers to a conversation that is going on in the background. Twitter and TodaysMeet are two popular tools written about in this book that allow you to create a back channel for use with your school/classroom.

Blogs—A blog (short for web log) is a website where a user or group of users writes or otherwise shares information and stories. Blog entries can be comprised of text, images, video, and anything else the author may use to help express their ideas.

Bookmarklet—A bookmarklet is a small shortcut that is saved into the bookmark bar of your web browser that allows you to quickly do a task. For example, you can click on a bookmarklet and automate the capture of web content to import into another website/tool.

BYOD—BYOD (bring your own device) is the idea that students and teachers can bring their own devices to school instead of relying on the school to supply a specific machine for all to use.

COPPA—COPPA (Children's Online Privacy Protection Act) was originally written in 1998 and put into effect in 2000, long before the social web. In 2012, the act was revised and better reflects the modern web landscape. The act aims to limit the information students can share with web services. This is one of the many misunderstood or misinterpreted laws cited when sites are blocked from classroom settings. You can read more information on the COPPA website.

Cloud—The Cloud commonly refers to the idea that the work you create on the Internet is saved and called from the Internet instead of on a specific machine.

Curation—Curation is the art of collecting and organizing content on the web. This can be anything from web links to images or any other content you are curating. Curation occurs either for oneself or for the community at large.

Digital Portfolio—A digital portfolio is a place where people (usually students) store examples of their work. Instead of showcasing numerical grades as achievements, these digital portfolios allow actual work samples in the form of websites, created content from various web tools, and images and text to tell the story of the work product.

Direct Message—A direct message (DM) is a private message sent between two users that follow one another on Twitter. There is no public record of the message being sent, but the sender and receiver can have a private conversation using this tool. One must be followed by the user they wish to DM in order for the message to be received.

Embed/Embedded—Embed means to place within. Embedded content is content that is housed elsewhere on the web, but able to be accessed with another web-page or web project. For example, YouTube offers options for embedding their videos on other sites. You can used the embed code (HTML code that tells the website how and what to capture from their site) to display a video on your site that is stored in and plays from YouTube's servers.

Flash—Flash is a popular animation language produced by Adobe. In order to work with sites or services that require Flash, a free download is necessary. While it is very popular and allows for many different kinds of interaction, Flash is not compatible for all devices, notably the iPad/iPod/iPhone.

Following—Following is a term that means you are signed up to receive and view another member's content on a site. For example, I follow you on Twitter in order to see your tweets in my feed.

Freemium—Freemium refers to the idea that websites offer most of their site for free, but have some premium features available for users to pay for. These members who pay for features offset the costs for the rest of the site's users. This is a common model for web tools in the education space.

Hashtag—Hashtag is a way to tag a word in a message so that it can be indexed and easily searched. This consists of a word within the message prefixed with a hash sign (#). For example, "#EdChat."

Infographics—Infographics are ways to take complex ideas or large quantities of data and display them in a more simple and visual manner. Infographics, as the name suggests, use a lot of graphics or pictures to help present the information.

JPEG—JPEG and its file extension JPG is a type of graphics compression. This is a very common file type that is usable by most programs for importing and exporting images. If you really want to know, it stands for Joint Photographic Experts Group.

Microblog—A microblog is, as the name implies, a blog on which the user can post brief bursts of information or updates on one's activities. Twitter is defined as a microblog because of the 140-character limitations in the tweet.

Personal Learning Network—Personal learning network (PLN) refers to the people whom you are connected to. It usually refers to a social network like Twitter or Edmodo.

PNG—PNG, which stands for portable network graphics, is a popular graphic extension. One notable benefit of PNG files is that they can maintain a layer of transparent backgrounds that make them easy to manipulate on graphic websites.

QR Codes—A QR code is a special kind of barcode readable by a computer scanner or application. Smartphones and cell phone cameras are the most common scanners of these codes, which consist of black modules arranged in a square pattern on a white background. The information encoded can lead the user to a website, video, text, etc.

Social Bookmarking—Social bookmarking refers to a concept where people can share their bookmarks (links to favorite sites and resources) with one another.

Tweets—The 140-character messages sent using the Twitter network.

Tweet-Up—Tweet-ups are meetings where you can meet your Twitter contacts face-to-face. Oftentimes, conferences related to education technology host tweet-up events that are great fun as well as a nice way to connect with the folks you are following.

URL—A URL (universal or uniform reference locator) is the address of the unique website page.

VoIP—VoIP (voice-over Internet protocol) refers to the transfer of voice over the Internet. Services like Skype or Vonage are two examples of popular tools that transmit voice/video over an Internet connection. This allows two parties with the software to connect without paying for a specific phone call.

Web 2.0—Web 2.0 refers to any site that you can interact with in a way to provide comments and ratings in addition to the use of a site to create new content. Most sites in the past five years are interactive and have some if not all the elements of what was called "Web 2.0."

Word Cloud—A word cloud (sometimes called a "tag cloud") is a graphic made of text usually created to show the content of a passage of text. Words are represented in various sizes with the largest words being the ones that repeat most frequently in the passage.

INDEX

CORWIN

A SAGE Company

The Corwin logo—a raven striding across an open book—represents the union of courage and learning. Corwin is committed to improving education for all learners by publishing books and other professional development resources for those serving the field of PreK–12 education. By providing practical, hands-on materials, Corwin continues to carry out the promise of its motto: **"Helping Educators Do Their Work Better."**